VANCOUVER
ISLAND
RAILROADS

This painting depicts the morning E&N passenger train steaming northbound over the Malahat at Arbutus Canyon in January 1946. It is based on a photo taken by my late friend, John Newman. John, a meticulous photographer, took many beautiful portraits of the E&N, but those at Arbutus, with its many moods of light and shadow, were probably his favourites and mine as well.—Robert D. Turner

VANCOUVER ISLAND RAILROADS

Robert D. Turner

Library of Congress Catalog Number
(first edition)
HE2809.V35T87 385'0911'34 72-95484

Canadian Cataloguing in Publication Data

Turner, Robert, D., 1947-
Vancouver Island Railroads

Includes bibliographical references and index.

ISBN 1-55039-083-X (bound) – ISBN 1-55039-077-5 (pbk.)

Railroads—British Columbia—Vancouver Island—History—I. Title.
HE2809.V35T87 1997 385'.09711'2 C97-910686-9

First Edition, 1973 (five printings) Golden West Books, California
Second Edition, 1997 (First Canadian Edition)
Second Printing: May 2005

Sono Nis Press most gratefully acknowledges the support for our publishing program provided by the Government of Canada through the Book Publishing Industry Development Program (BPIDP), the Canada Council for the Arts, and the British Columbia Arts Council.

Jacket Illustration: Robert D. Turner

Published by
Sono Nis Press
PO Box 160
Winlaw, BC V0G 2J0
Canada

1-800-370-5228 (North America)
250-226-0077 (International)

books@sononis.com
www.sononis.com

Printed and bound in Canada by Kromar Printing.

To Nancy

ACKNOWLEDGEMENTS

LARGE PORTIONS of any history are based on events beyond an author's direct experience, and it is only through the work of a few far sighted and interested individuals that the material essential for the preparation of a book such as this has been collected and preserved over the last century.

I am deeply indebted to the following people for the loan of illustrative material and for sharing with me their recollections and experiences. They are: Earl Barlow, Gerald M. Best, Herbert L. Broadbelt, H. J. (Bob) Brown, Dominique Coumont, Ronald D'Altroy, Harre Demoro, Albert Farrow, Norman Gidney, Fred Hall, W. Hasanen, A. J. Helmcken, Mrs. G. Hodgeson, John Hoffmeister, Fred Holm, Rick Horne, Bill and Dorothy Johnstone, Jack Kennedy, R. J. Knight, P. H. LeMare, John Lockner, A. B. McNeill, Bill Mellon, John Newman, Albert H. Paull, Ted Robson, Stan F. Styles, Ernie Timperley, Elwood White and Dave Wilkie.

In addition, sincere thanks and appreciation are extended to the following organizations and companies for their assistance. They are: British Columbia Department of Commercial Transport, British Columbia Department of Travel Industry, British Columbia Forest Products, British Columbia Forest Service, British Columbia Hydro & Power Authority, British Columbia Provincial Library, Cam's Photo Service, Canadian Forest Products Limited, Canadian National Railways, Canadian Pacific Railway, Crown Zellerbach Canada Ltd., MacMillan Bloedel Ltd., Nanaimo Centennial Museum, University of British Columbia Library, Vancouver Public Library and Victoria Press Ltd.

Appreciation is extended to the British Columbia Provincial Archives (now the British Columbia Archives) in Victoria for their outstanding efforts to collect and preserve photographic and documentary records of the early days of the history of the province. Special credit must also be given to the late Leonard Frank, a pioneering photographer in British Columbia, whose work appears throughout this book. Through the generosity of the late O. F. Landauer of Leonard Frank Photos, the vast collection of historical photographs taken by Mr. Frank has been donated to the Vancouver Public Library. Finally, a special word of thanks goes to my cousin Mark Horne, my brother Bill and my wife Nancy.

The first edition of this book was published in 1973 by Golden West Books in San Marino, California. My sincere thanks go to publisher Donald Duke for his advice and many contributions including the design for the original book and for his cooperation with the second edition. Diane Morriss and Ann West of Sono Nis Press made the second edition possible and it has been a pleasure to work with them to see the book back in print. Bev Leech designed the new cover and the additional sections as well as contributed in many ways to the project.

During the 25 years since the original text and the acknowledgements above were written much has changed on Vancouver Island and many more people have helped me on writing and research projects. Most have been acknowledged in my subsequent books but a special thanks must go to Barry Volkers, Dave Wilkie and the late Gerry Wellburn. Too many old friends, including many of the people acknowledged here, have passed on. For this second edition, my friends Dave Wilkie and Peter Corley-Smith and my wife Nancy read the new material and I am very grateful for their information and advice. Dave also contributed more of his beautiful photography.

Throughout North America, the use of steam power faded rapidly in the years following the Second World War. On Vancouver Island, the Esquimalt and Nanaimo dieselized its operations completely in 1949 but Canadian National remained a stronghold for steam until 1958 when diesels finally took over from the small stable of 2-8-0s and other light locomotives based in Victoria. Dave Wilkie captured CN's 2128 on Train 587 leaving Tyup, near Cowichan Bay, on a cold and snowy January 28, 1957. (LEFT) In beautiful spring weather, the 2099 works Victoria-bound Train 586 over the trestle at Mile 21.0 on May 14, 1957.—BOTH DAVE WILKIE

Dave Wilkie is a tireless photographer of Vancouver Island's railroads and his work has captured almost every facet of their changing story over the last half century. These two early colour photos of the CNR are the first of many of Dave's pictures that follow. It is particularly gratifying to include more of his work in the second edition. —RDT

PREFACE

VANCOUVER ISLAND, on the west coast of British Columbia, has been the site of railroading for nearly 140 years. Few places of comparable area have had the diversity of equipment and operation that has prevailed on Vancouver Island. On an island just over 300 miles (480 km) long and averaging about 70 miles (110 km) in width, there have been numerous logging and mining railways, an electric interurban and streetcar system, shortlines, construction railways and the branch lines of two major transcontinentals.

The island has provided a spectacular setting for these operations. Running the full length of Vancouver Island, in a north-south direction, is a series of rugged mountain ranges. Showing the effects of recent continental and alpine glaciation, the ranges are characterized by many sharply pointed peaks, steep-sided valleys and rounded foothills. While few peaks rise above 7,000 feet (2000 m), most are within 20 miles (30 km) of the sea coast. As a result, their slopes are steep and they are as spectacular and scenic as mountains of much greater elevation.

On the west coast of Vancouver Island, the topography is extremely rugged. The land drops steeply into the sea, and many deep inlets penetrate well back into the interior. Along the southeast coast of the island is a long narrow coastal plain, typified by low rolling hills and flat bottom lands. These merge at several points with east west valleys that provide the only major passes through the central ranges.

Vancouver Island's climate is generally mild. Except in alpine areas, the average monthly temperatures seldom fall below freezing and rarely rise above 80 degrees Fahrenheit (26 degrees C) in the summer. Annual rainfall ranges from about 30 inches (75 cm) in the Victoria area at the southern tip of the island to well over 200 inches (500 cm) on the west coast.

Different precipitation levels and topography in various parts of the island result in notable differences in vegetation. The west coast temperate rain forests are dominated by dense stands of western hemlock, Sitka spruce, amabilis fir and western redcedar. East of the mountains, where the rainfall seldom exceeds 70 inches (180 cm) a year, the most abundant species is Douglas-fir. The vast forests formed a thick blanket extending from the coast up to timberline at about 3,500 feet (1100 m). The mature, old-growth trees reached giant proportions. Cedars often reached 10-15 feet (3-5 m) in diameter at the base; exceptional Spruce and Douglas-fir could tower over 300 feet (90 m) in height with the lower trunks clear of branches for 100 feet (30 m) or more. Thousands of acres were covered with trees hundreds of years old, containing some of the world's finest softwoods. Logs typically were three to five feet (1-1.5 m) in diameter.

The first European settlers, arriving in British Columbia in the mid-1800's, were mainly interested in farming the rich lowland soils. They found the vast forests a hindrance and very difficult to clear. Often logging was encouraged before settlement in areas such as the Comox Valley and the Saanich Peninsula.

The beauty and richness of Vancouver Island were widely advertised to encourage settlers and immigrants to move to the west coast. As a result, hundreds of settlers, mainly from the British Isles, flocked to Vancouver Island each year. The centers of Victoria and Nanaimo, originally established as trading posts and forts by the Hudson's Bay Company, grew rapidly into bustling communities.

High over Bear Creek on one of the most spectacular wooden bridges in the west, a British Columbia Forest Products Ltd. Shay locomotive eases an impressive trainload of timber from Vancouver Island's interior mountains to tidewater on the Pacific. — GOLDEN WEST COLLECTION

Situated in the beautiful Nimpkish Valley of northern Vancouver Island, Canadian Forest Products Ltd.'s isolated Woss Camp is a center for the last logging railway operation in Canada. The cut over lowlands, patch-work patterns of roads, orderly camp, and high wooden railway trestle mark the influence of logging on the landscape of rugged mountain ranges and forested, steep-sided valleys, typical of most of British Columbia's Vancouver Island.—CANFOR

In rugged relief, Vancouver Island stands out against the mountainous coastline of British Columbia and the Olympic Peninsula of Washington State. This illustration was prepared from a photograph of a map carved from wood by David Murdoch. The relief is exaggerated by a factor of eight for visual presentation.—ROBERT D. TURNER

STEAM

The last stand of steam power in regular service on Vancouver Island, except where locomotives were used as mill switchers, was MacMillan Bloedel's log hauling operation from the Nanaimo Lakes to Ladysmith and at the log dump and mill at Chemainus. The inevitable came in December 1969 when the last logs were dumped at Chemainus. No. 1055 was retained as a mill switcher until 1973. Eventually, all four of MacMillan Bloedel's last steam locomotives were preserved. These scenes show the 1055 arriving at Ladysmith on December 19, 1968 and, on February 18, 1969, about to leave for the woods. (RIGHT) At Chemainus, No. 1044 works a cut of empty skeleton cars up the switchback to the E&N interchange in December 1968.—ALL ROBERT D. TURNER

McMILLAN & BLOEDEL LTD
1044

The discovery of workable coal deposits near the coast at Fort Rupert, Nanaimo, Wellington and later Cumberland, and around Ladysmith, prompted further immigration as miners were brought in or moved to the coast from England, Scotland, China, Japan and elsewhere. Agriculture flourished at Duncan, on the Saanich Peninsula and in the Comox Valley. At the same time a forest industry was developing; the seemingly endless stands of huge timber proved to be more valuable than any mining bonanza. Sawmilling, slow at first to develop because of limited markets and the difficulties of handling the large timbers, gathered importance at Port Alberni, Sooke, Victoria, Chemainus, Ladysmith, Nanaimo, Campbell River, Courtenay and many other locations. In time, other communities were formed and some of the original ones declined in importance. Victoria, as the provincial capital, grew into a major center that boasted a harbour surrounded by steamer docks, mills and shipyards. By the late 1990's, although Victoria's population was nearly 320,000, the traditional resource-industry economy had all but disappeared.

Railways came early to Vancouver Island. The development of the Nanaimo coal mines necessitated the construction of a short standard gauge mining railroad, so that many years before the rails of the famed Canadian Pacific Railway reached British Columbia, active railroading was proceeding at the settlement of Nanaimo. This was the first of several mining railroads to operate in the district. Mining for metals had little impact on railroad development. Only one small railroad, the narrow gauge Lenora, Mt. Sicker Railway was built expressly to handle ore.

In the pioneering economy of 19th century Vancouver Island, railroads were looked upon as the best means of taming the wilderness. Many elaborate schemes were promoted for the development of railways through every conceivable pass on Vancouver Island, and local residents fought a losing battle with the Federal Government to have Victoria made the western terminus of the Canadian Pacific Railway. As the population of Vancouver Island grew, railroads were built along the east coast where the major settlements were located. By 1911, a line also had been extended to the west coast at Alberni and in 1914 rails reached north to Courtenay on the east coast.

The massive forests provided a major incentive for the construction of railroads on the Island. From tentative beginnings along the east coast at Chemainus, Ladysmith, around Shawnigan Lake and near Nanaimo, railroad logging expanded rapidly in the early 1900's until many large scale operations were providing a key link in the development of an export-oriented sawmilling industry. Rail logging was carried out on a large scale for over half a century on Vancouver Island, finally giving way to truck logging in the 1950's. By that time, the logging railways had been a major instrument of change and had been used to log the lowlands of most of the major valleys on southern and eastern Vancouver Island. The railways and the steam donkeys used in the woods were probably the single most important means of removing the old growth forests from the eastern side of the Island in the areas adjacent to the Gulf of Georgia. This huge, sheltered inland waterway became almost a mill pond for the intense logging of the forests in southwestern British Columbia. Hundreds of tugs towed thousands of log booms from the railroad log dumps to mills on Vancouver Island and to centers on the mainland. Only three logging railways survived into the 1960's and by the 1990's, only one remained.

Vancouver Island has changed dramatically in the last 25 years since *Vancouver Island Railroads* was first published. The population has grown substantially, urbanization has accelerated and the transportation systems and industrial base of the island have been altered significantly. Victoria has grown tremendously in population in the last quarter century. By 1996 the regional population had grown from 200,000 in the early 1970's to nearly 320,000. The east coast of the island experienced similar changes. At the same time, the economy has changed dramatically. Victoria witnessed the disappearance of nearly all traditional industries that had once provided steady traffic for the railways. Industrial areas around the harbour served by either the E&N or the CNR have become sites for hotels and condominiums. Waterfront walkways have replaced industrial trackage. In many island communities the forest-based economy declined as the timber supply dwindled and mills closed. Consumer goods and many other products once shipped to the island by rail are now nearly all handled by trucks and containers operating from mainland warehouses and intermodal terminals. Railways on Vancouver Island have not done well in the face of these changes and the last 25 years have most often been a time of decline and abandonment.

Victoria, with its growing population, increasing traffic congestion and limited downtown core, still has an opportunity to develop a light rail or suburban rail system as a tool in directing and focusing regional

growth. However, as highway construction and suburbanization proceed, the options become less flexible and more difficult to implement. Although light rail transit systems have been proposed for many years, only studies and very long range plans have been made. Heritage streetcars for the Inner Harbour area have also been discussed but no substantive action has followed.

There are also exciting possibilities for the development of heritage rail operations on Vancouver Island. For example, the scenic CPR route over the Malahat Range north of Victoria is a natural setting for summer tourist-oriented services. Such developments can be a key to maintaining the quality of environment so often associated with Vancouver Island.

In this new edition of *Vancouver Island Railroads*, the text and nearly all illustrations have been retained in their original form, reflecting the state of operations in the early 1970's. To bring this survey of the Island's railways up to date, a few corrections and amendments have been made within the text and a new chapter, as well as this expanded preface, have been added to highlight the changes to Vancouver Island's surviving rail lines in the last quarter century.

Robert D. Turner

The E&N's Niagara Canyon bridge, shown above in 1973, is an engineering landmark in Canada. The cast-iron and steel cantilever bridge was built over the Fraser River at Cisco in the Fraser Canyon in 1884. Fabricated in England by Hawks, Crawshay, and Co. of Gateshead-on-Tyne, to the designs of Charles Conrad Schneider, it was erected by the San Francisco Bridge Company as part of the Onderdonk contracts for CPR construction. In late 1910, it was moved to Niagara for reassembly to replace the huge wooden trestle that had served the line since the 1880's. Towering masonry piers support the 529-foot span 260 feet above the stream bed. Niagara is the oldest cantilever railroad bridge in operation and it was the second built. —ROBERT D. TURNER

(BELOW) Highway construction north of Victoria, shown on July 23, 1997, required four new railway bridges but also symbolized the change away from rail transport on Vancouver Island. —DAVE WILKIE

8009

8009
8009

TRESTLES & BALDWINS

The Esquimalt and Nanaimo's Baldwin roadswitchers served on Vancouver Island for nearly a quarter century. They were classic first generation diesel power and pioneered the use of diesels in main line service on the Canadian Pacific. The 1,000-hp locomotives, often used in conjunction with Baldwin switchers, were equipped for multi-unit operations in their later years and as many as four units were needed on heavy trains to and from Port Alberni and occasionally to Victoria. The Alberni line featured a spectacular series of wooden trestles along Cameron Lake and west to Port Alberni. (LEFT) The 8009 heads two other 8000s eastbound over the trestle at Mile 27.3 on September 28, 1968. (BELOW LEFT) The year before, on November 25, 1967, the 8009 leads two units and 35 loads from Port Alberni upgrade over the trestle at Mile 25. (RIGHT) Fifty cars required the power of the 8008, 8003, 8002 and 8007 to pull this train from Port Alberni over Locharkaig Summit on March 30, 1968. This trestle, at Mile 23.9, was bypassed in 1971. (BELOW) Two roadswitchers, once again with the 8009 in the lead, and a yard unit cross one of the large trestles along beautiful Cameron Lake on November 25, 1967.—ALL DAVE WILKIE

Niagara Canyon on the Esquimalt and Nanaimo Railway's scenic line along the east coast of Vancouver Island has been a highlight of the railway since the construction days of the mid-1880's. In this photograph, a spotless locomotive No. 914 is wheeling a five-car passenger train upgrade towards Malahat Station, the summit of the climb north of Victoria. It is a crisp November morning in 1945.—John Newman

CONTENTS

Efficient transportation was the key to developing the coal mines on Vancouver Island and railroads provided the vital link between the mines and the ships used to carry Vancouver Island coal to San Francisco and other important markets. Here, six windjammers crowd the deep sea wharves of the Union Colliery Company at Union Bay. This operation came into production in the late 1880's and was the last major coal producer on the Island when it closed down in 1960. — Provincial Archives

1

MINING RAILROADS

VANCOUVER ISLAND'S eastern coastal plain is underlain by thick beds of sedimentary rock deposited over a period of millions of years. Interspersed between the layers of sandstones, shales, and conglomerates that comprise these formations are a number of thick beds of high quality bituminous coal. These coal beds are concentrated in three principal areas. One deposit occurs at Fort Rupert, near the northern tip of Vancouver Island, while a second major concentration is located in the Comox region. The best known seams are found further south in the Wellington-Ladysmith district near the city of Nanaimo. For over a century, the coal at these three sites provided the basis for some of the most lucrative colliery operations in western North America.

In the mid-1800's, the Hudson's Bay Company began to develop the newly discovered coal deposits at Fort Rupert. Seeing opportunities on Vancouver Island that did not present themselves in Europe, a young Scottish mining engineer named Robert Dunsmuir emigrated from Scotland with his wife and two young daughters in December 1850, to take a position with the Hudson's Bay Company at the new mines. They sailed from Kilmarnock, Scotland, aboard the ship *Pekin,* but were delayed in reaching Vancouver Island when their ship grounded at the mouth of the Columbia River en route to the Hudson's Bay Company's Fort Vancouver (now Vancouver, Washington). They were delayed there for three months, and meanwhile a son, James, was born on July 8. When the family was ready to travel again, they continued north, arriving at Fort Rupert in September 1851. Dunsmuir had been working at the Fort Rupert mine only a short time when it was realized that the coal seam was broken and that it would become increasingly difficult and costly to extract the coal.

Meanwhile, coal had been discovered by Indians in the Nanaimo area. They were unaware of its potential value and had shown the location of some of the outcroppings to Hudson's Bay Company officials at Fort Victoria (now Victoria). Development work commenced almost immediately. The initial mining operations were primitive. The coal was transported by dugout canoe out to the ships in the harbour, where it was loaded into lighters and shovelled on board. The first shipments left Nanaimo in September 1852 aboard the steamer *Caribou,* bound for Victoria.

In 1854, the Fort Rupert mine was closed down and the Dunsmuirs moved to Nanaimo, where Robert began working in the new mines. By this time, a second son, Alex, had been born. In 1861, the Hudson's Bay Company sold its mining inter-

Robert Dunsmuir came to Vancouver Island in 1851 and in the next 38 years developed the largest coal mines on the Island, built the Esquimalt and Nanaimo Railway, and became one of British Columbia's leading industrial and political figures. (BELOW) The Island's first railroad was operated by the Vancouver Coal Mining and Land Company at Nanaimo. Here the locomotive *London* nears the docks with a loaded coal train while the *Pioneer* steams in the background. — BOTH PROVINCIAL ARCHIVES

ests to an English firm, which formed the Vancouver Coal Mining and Land Company. The new owners soon recognized the necessity of increasing the efficiency of the coal-loading facilities. They decided to build a small standard gauge railroad from the mines to newly constructed loading wharves in Nanaimo Harbour.

In 1863, the first locomotive for the railway arrived from England and was immediately placed in service hauling coal to the shipping wharves. Christened the *Pioneer*, the machine was a typical ten ton English industrial locomotive with an open cab, 8 by 10-inch cylinders and boiler pressure of 115 pounds. Modest as it was, *Pioneer* soon proved its worth.

At the company's first annual meeting, held in March 1864, the directors reported that the locomotive, which was the first to operate in Canada west of Ontario, had already substantially reduced the costs of handling the coal. They expected production to rise significantly as soon as new rail and more equipment could be added to the railroad. In 1866 a second locomotive, similar to the first but smaller, was ordered from England. This machine was named the *Euclawtaw* after an Indian group from the Campbell River area which, according to one account, lost a tug-of-war contest with the new engine on its arrival at Nanaimo.

By this time other coal mines were beginning to open up around Nanaimo. Robert Dunsmuir had left his job with the Vancouver Coal Mining and Land Company to work for the new Harewood

This early scene along the Nanaimo waterfront shows two of the four British built tank locomotives operated at Nanaimo on the railway of the Vancouver Coal Mining and Land Company. The large No. 1 Mine may be seen in the distance. — PROVINCIAL ARCHIVES

Coal Company. This was a smaller operation than the one carried out by his former employers. Dunsmuir was hired by the Harewood Company to prospect its lands to determine the extent of its coal deposits. The company had ambitious plans for development of the coal seam. It planned to construct a railroad to Departure Bay, and application was made to the Provincial Government for a charter. This was granted, but it stipulated that the railroad had to be completed by April 1866. The company found it necessary to apply for an extension, but before work commenced, Captain Horace Lascelles, the owner of the property, died. With his death, prospects for immediate development passed and the property was sold.

In 1869, the future of the Dunsmuir family looked brighter. Dunsmuir often had visions of a more prosperous future than could be attained by working as a mining engineer for the rest of his life. He had spent many weekends exploring the Nanaimo district and found several coal outcroppings. However, he bided his time until he could discover a really rich and workable deposit. One day, while on a fishing trip to Diver Lake near the present site of Wellington, his long search was rewarded by the discovery of a rich coal seam. Not one to act in haste, Dunsmuir checked out the new prospect carefully before embarking on any development work. The coal was found to be the best of any discovered on the west coast of North America, and Dunsmuir was assured a ready sale at the principal market place of San Francisco. Unable to raise sufficient capital for the development works by himself, he entered into partnership in 1871 with Lieutenant Diggle of the Royal Navy, forming Dunsmuir, Diggle and Company. Two years later, in order to gain further backing for the development of the mines, they expanded the partnership to include Admiral Farquhar and Captain Egerton, also Royal Navy Officers. The three officers invested about $150,000 in the development of the mines, and in return were given half interest in the property. Dunsmuir, however, retained control over the company's operations.

The new mines were located close to the protected harbour of Departure Bay, just north of Nanaimo. This was found to be an ideal shipping point for the mines, and as soon as transport facilities were ready, the first shipment of Wellington coal left Departure Bay aboard the ship, *Caesarewich*, bound for San Francisco. Initially, the coal was hauled to Departure Bay in wagons drawn by horses and mules. However, the capacity of this method was limited and it soon became necessary to establish a more efficient transportation system. A 2-foot 6-inch gauge tramway was then built between the mines and Departure Bay. Until steel rail could be imported from England, 4 by 4-inch timbers, strapped with iron, were used on the line. Because of the grade encountered, a gravity incline was employed in the operation. This incline was about 1,000 yards in length and had a grade of approximately 5.5 percent. Loaded cars were lowered by cable, at the same time pulling the light empty cars back towards the mines. At the Departure Bay docks and in the small yards around the mines, mules were used to switch the cars.

In 1874, Lieutenant Diggle purchased the first locomotives for the railroad. They were two traction engines owned by the British Admiralty, which were converted to locomotives on their arrival at Departure Bay by the addition of flanged wheels. The acquisition of these two machines greatly accelerated the production of the mines.

By the early 1870's, Dunsmuir's two sons were becoming involved in the workings of the company. James, along with John Bryden, managed the works at Wellington, while Alex assisted with company business in Victoria. Assured of financial success, Dunsmuir moved his family to a newly built home, named *Ardoon*, at Wellington. Soon after, James left Vancouver Island to continue his training at the Willamette Iron Works in Portland. Here he became a qualified machinist. Later he was to attend the Hamilton Military Academy at Blackburg, Virginia, to complete his education, before returning to Vancouver Island to settle in Wellington. At the prompting of Alex the company set up offices in San Francisco in order to manage the sale of coal more efficiently. In later years, Alex became a resident manager of these offices.

As production increased in the mines, it became necessary to expand the original railway system. To this end, two new locomotives were ordered from the Baldwin Locomotive Works in Philadelphia. The first of these, the *Duke*, had been seen by Robert Dunsmuir in 1876 at the American Centennial Exhibition. It arrived at Departure Bay aboard the ship *Washington Libby*, in 1878. It was soon followed by the nearly identical *Duch-*

On the left, Robert Dunsmuir sporting a shiny stovepipe hat, poses beside his locomotive *Duchess* as a Wellington Colliery Railway train prepares to leave Wellington for Departure Bay. The second woman to the right of Dunsmuir is his wife Joan. Also note the Indian and Chinese miners riding the train. (BELOW) The Wellington Colliery Railway's Departure Bay docks as they appeared in the 1890's. In the foreground is one of the 0-6-0 tank locomotives with a coal train from Wellington.—Both Provincial Archives

Polished and gleaming, the *Victoria* stands ready to leave the Baldwin Locomotive Works plant in Philadelphia. Bearing construction number 9869, the 0-6-0 was built in 1889 and operated for Dunsmuir and his successors until 1952 when it was placed on display at Nanaimo. — H. L. BROADBELT COLLECTION

ess. Both machines were 0-6-0 saddle tankers with 10 by 12-inch cylinders and 42-inch drivers. Originally they were built to 2-foot 6-inch gauge, but were widened in later years as the railroad operation was upgraded. The *Duchess* was usually assigned to the Departure Bay wharves, while the *Duke* worked the yards at Wellington. Soon after these engines were acquired, Dunsmuir felt himself able to buy out the shares of Admiral Farquhar and Lieutenant Egerton.

In 1879, Dunsmuir, Diggle and Company purchased the holdings of the South Wellington Colliery Company which had been developing since 1876 just south of the Dunsmuir operations. The acquisition of this property removed the possible threat of a major competitor developing on Dunsmuir's doorstep and expanded the opportunities available for further work on the Wellington mines.

The South Wellington Colliery was well developed. At the time of the purchase, it had two shafts in operation and a modern operating three-foot gauge railroad running from the mines to Departure Bay. Rolling stock included a newly acquired Baldwin built tank locomotive which had arrived from San Francisco in August 1878 aboard the barque *Don Nichlas* and several dozen coal cars or "waggons." Although it was well developed physically, the South Wellington Colliery had never been able to become financially stable. In 1877, it was barely saved from financial collapse by mining promoter R. D. Chandler, a backer of the company, who paid off disgruntled miners on the verge of leaving the diggings. Nevertheless, conditions continued to deteriorate, and in March of the following year, the mine was declared insolvent and work stopped. The entire operation was placed up for public auction, and was acquired by Chandler, who renewed the working of the mine. He improved the railroad and ordered a new stationary engine for the mine, but all to no avail. When he was faced with the $.75 per ton tariff on coal entering San Francisco, Chandler found he could not compete sucessfully with the larger Wellington and Nanaimo Collieries. After the sale of the entire operation to Dunsmuir, Diggle and Company, the South Wellington mine became the *Adit Level* of Dunsmuir's mines and the two railroads were connected using sections of dual gauge trackage.

During the winter of 1879, Dunsmuir replaced the old gravity incline by rerouting sections of the railway, making it possible for the locomotives to haul trains directly from the pitheads at Wellington to Departure Bay. Engines passed at the foot of the abandoned incline, with their 50-ton trains, making a round trip in about an hour. While it is not confirmed, it appears that Dunsmuir took this opportunity to rebuild his original 2-foot 6-inch gauge line to 3-foot gauge, thus obtaining an integration of the two narrow gauge systems. Use of the South Wellington docks was soon discontinued, and the line of the South Wellington Colliery's railway was eventually abandoned.

By 1880, production from the Wellington mines had risen to a new high of nearly 190,000 tons, over 162,000 tons of which were sold for export. An entire fleet of ships was kept busy transporting Dunsmuir coal down the coast to San Francisco. Among the ships regularly calling at Departure

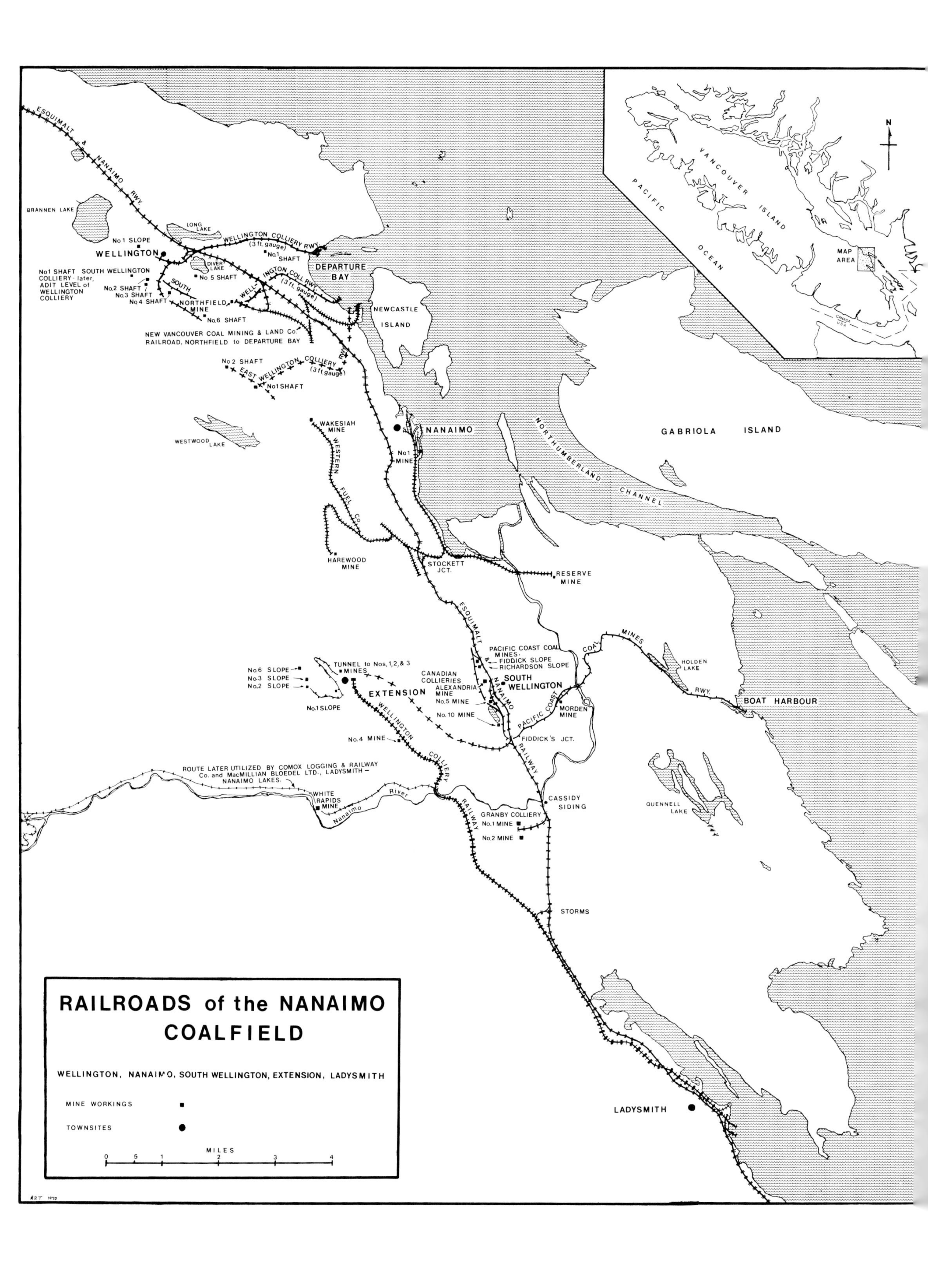

RAILROADS of the NANAIMO COALFIELD
WELLINGTON, NANAIMO, SOUTH WELLINGTON, EXTENSION, LADYSMITH
MINE WORKINGS
TOWNSITES
MILES
0
.5
1
2
3
4
ESQUIMALT & NANAIMO RWY.
BRANNEN LAKE
LONG LAKE
No 1 SLOPE
WELLINGTON
WELLINGTON COLLIERY RWY (3 ft.gauge)
No.1 SHAFT
DEPARTURE BAY
No1 SHAFT SOUTH WELLINGTON COLLIERY - later, ADIT LEVEL of WELLINGTON COLLIERY
DIVER LAKE
No. 5 SHAFT
No.2 SHAFT
No.3 SHAFT
No.4 SHAFT
SOUTH
NORTHFIELD MINE
No.6 SHAFT
WELLINGTON COLL RWY (3 ft. gauge)
NEWCASTLE ISLAND
NEW VANCOUVER COAL MINING & LAND Co. RAILROAD, NORTHFIELD to DEPARTURE BAY
No 2 SHAFT
EAST WELLINGTON COLLIERY RWY (3 ft.gauge)
No1 SHAFT
WAKESIAH MINE
NANAIMO
WESTWOOD LAKE
No 1 MINE
WESTERN FUEL Co.
NORTHUMBERLAND CHANNEL
GABRIOLA ISLAND
HAREWOOD MINE
STOCKETT JCT.
RESERVE MINE
ESQUIMALT
PACIFIC COAST COAL MINES, FIDDICK SLOPE
RICHARDSON SLOPE
No.6 SLOPE
No.3 SLOPE
No.2 SLOPE
No.1 SLOPE
TUNNEL to Nos. 1, 2, & 3 MINES
EXTENSION
CANADIAN COLLIERIES ALEXANDRIA MINE
No.5 MINE
No. 10 MINE
SOUTH WELLINGTON
NANAIMO
PACIFIC COAST
MORDEN MINE
COAL MINES RWY.
HOLDEN LAKE
BOAT HARBOUR
No.4 MINE
WELLINGTON COLLIERY RAILWAY
FIDDICK'S JCT.
RAILWAY
ROUTE LATER UTILIZED BY COMOX LOGGING & RAILWAY Co. and MacMILLIAN BLOEDEL LTD., LADYSMITH - NANAIMO LAKES.
WHITE RAPIDS MINE
Nanaimo River
CASSIDY SIDING
GRANBY COLLIERY
No.1 MINE
No.2 MINE
QUENNELL LAKE
STORMS
LADYSMITH
VANCOUVER ISLAND
PACIFIC OCEAN
MAP AREA
N
CANADA
USA
RDT 1970

Bay were the barques *Union, Remejao, Constitution, Wellington,* and *Edwin.* By this time, the railroad had grown into a sizable system. Dunsmuir reported to the Department of Mines in 1880 that he had five locomotives and 150 coal "waggons" in operation on his ten mile railroad. The current wage level for his workers was $2.00 to $3.75 per day for whites and $1.00 to $1.25 for Chinese doing the same work. Over 500 men were employed in the pits at this time.

In 1883, Dunsmuir was in a position to buy out his last partner. He paid Diggle nearly three quarters of a million dollars for his investment. At last Dunsmuir was his own master. The company was reincorporated under the name Robert Dunsmuir and Sons Limited, since both of Dunsmuir's sons were in a position to take an active role in the family business. Also in that year, the railroad was incorporated separately as the Wellington Colliery Railway. Five shafts were in operation by this time in the Wellington area, and export traffic continued at a high level.

At this time, further competition appeared when the East Wellington Colliery was opened to the southeast of Dunsmuir's mines. This company, owned by Chandler, the former owner of the South Wellington Colliery, began development of two shafts in the area, but trouble was encountered in locating the coal. The seams were interspersed with large amounts of rock and were very irregular. Nevertheless, a three and a half mile narrow gauge railroad was built from East Wellington to the south side of Departure Bay, where large ocean docks were constructed. The site of this terminal is presently occupied by British Columbia Ferries' Departure Bay docks. The company soon acquired two small Baldwin 0-6-0 tank locomotives for the new railroad. Interestingly, they were almost identical to those operated by Dunsmuir at his Wellington mines.

Chandler continued to search for the good coal that he was sure was located near his mines. In 1884, he shut down his eastern shaft and concentrated on the western mine, which was closer to Wellington and showed encouraging signs of producing a profitable seam. The coal soon evened out, averaging only about two feet in thickness, but it was of very high quality. Soon after, another shaft was opened. The company managed to produce over 28,000 tons of coal in 1886 and it continued to operate at a marginal level for the next decade.

Meanwhile, the Dunsmuirs, not content merely to collect the profits from the booming Wellington mines, became interested in the coal seams of the Comox area, about 100 miles north of Wellington. Here, coal had been discovered as early as 1853, and by the early 1870's several deposits of high

This early view of Cumberland shows the Union Colliery Railway's engine *Queen Ann* formerly the Central Pacific's No. 4, the *T. D. Judah*. Cumberland was a typical miners' shack town cut out of the forest with little thought for comfort or aesthetics. — Provincial Archives

grade coal had been described.

The first development of these seams was on a small scale. The Baynes Sound Colliery, incorporated in 1870, began mining operations along the Tsolum River. A small three and a half mile long narrow gauge railroad was built, and an eight ton Baldwin locomotive and about 25 cars were operated between the mine and the shipping point on Comox Harbour. However, the depressed coal market of 1876-77 brought about the closure of this small company and the mines were not reactivated.

Another small company to begin developing the coal deposits at Comox was the Union Bay Coal Company. A railway was graded to Royston on the coast, but an advanced stage of operation was never reached. By 1883, the Dunsmuirs had acquired all the major coal claims in the Comox area and began preparation for the large scale development of the coal field. However, Robert Dunsmuir's attention was being increasingly diverted from the colliery operations by his developing political career. This was especially true after his election to the Provincial Legislature as Member for Nanaimo in 1882. Accordingly, James became more and more involved in the management of the company. Also at this time, Robert was studying a proposal to build a railroad from Victoria to Nanaimo. He made the decision to undertake this project, and as partial payment, received title to the vast Esquimalt and Nanaimo Land Grant. The story of the construction of this railway, the Esquimalt and Nanaimo, is detailed in the following chapter. When this railway was completed in late 1886, the Dunsmuirs began the actual development of the Comox coal field. Work commenced under the name of the Union Colliery Company, with James Dunsmuir as managing director and later president. By 1888, the company's No. 1 and No. 2 Mines were in production. Eleven miles of standard gauge railway were constructed from the mines, near the site of Cumberland, to the coast. The railroad paralleled the Trent River to a point about one mile inland, where it crossed the river over a high wooden trestle and dropped to the terminus at Union Bay. Here, large shops, coke ovens, and deep sea wharves were built.

The first locomotive used on the new railway was an unusual machine, with a 4-2-2 wheel arrangement. It was acquired from the Central Pacific Railroad in California, where it had operated

Cumberland's Chinatown was at its height when this photograph was taken about 1900. Today little remains of this once busy community. — Provincial Archives

as the *T. D. Judah,* their No. 4. Built in 1863 by Danforth-Cooke, it was the second oldest steam locomotive to operate on Vancouver Island. It was only one year younger than the Vancouver Coal Mining and Land Company's little *Pioneer.* The locomotive was not at all suited to work at the mines. Its two large driving wheels and small cylinders could not produce sufficient tractive effort to work the heavy coal trains from the mines to Union Bay. After heavier machines were acquired, the *Queen Ann* or alternately *Betsey Jane,* as it was called, was relegated to yard work at Union Bay and was eventually scrapped in 1912.

In January 1888, the inevitable occurred — a gas explosion rocked the No. 5 pit at Wellington. In the Department of Mines Report for 1889 the sad details were related:

> This is the pit belonging to Messrs. Robert Dunsmuir and Sons, to which there is a branch line from the Esquimalt and Nanaimo Railway so that the railway company's locomotives go under the shute at the pit for their own supply of coal. From the pit also trains of cars loaded with coal are dispatched to Victoria.
>
> In this mine all things went as usual, until the 24th of January of last year when the workmen on the surface became suddenly aware that a terrible explosion had taken place in the mine, where 168 men were then engaged below. The working of the hoisting cage was stopped by the force of the explosion, and nothing was heard from any person below for quite a time after. The covering of the fan-shaft was also broken. This was, however, with all speed temporarily repaired and the fan kept running to its full speed, so that where it was possible, pure air might be got into the workings, until such time as help could go down from the top.

After a communication was got with those below, it was encouraging to know that there were a great many men in the bottom waiting to be taken up, and this was done with after an unavoidable delay of nearly three hours. As the men came up, enquiry was made as to where the explosion had taken place, but no one could tell. There were men brought up that came from the slope and the west side, but none of the men from the east side came up, and nothing was known of them. As none of the men that worked in the east side were sent up, it was certain that that was the place or division of the mine in which the explosion had taken place. This conclusion, afterwards, proved too true, as after all the men that were in bottom of the shaft were got out to the number 91 (ninety-one), there were yet 31 (thirty-one) white men and 46 Chinese missing, and from the condition of the ventilation of the mine it was plain that it was not possible for any of the men in the east side or level to be got out alive, but at the same time there was no want of men to go down to see if they could get some out; not one, however, of those that were in the east level was left alive to tell the tale. There was only one injured got out, and he was near the bottom of the shaft.

As it was impossible to get far into the workings, owing to the after-damp being so strong, air had to be taken in as we went along, and the bodies got out as could be got at; so that by noon of the 26th of January, the bodies of all the white men and 37 Chinese were got out, leaving yet 9 Chinese to be accounted for, and those were got out from time to time as the mine was cleaned up, when on the 9th day of May, the last body was got out making 77 deaths; and in my opinion, it was owing to their being able to keep the fan running, which kept the after-damp from the downcast shaft, that the 91 men who were got out alive were saved.

As I have observed, previous to the explosion everything in and about the mine was in good order, nothing seemed lacking. This mine, before the explosion, was the best ventilated in the district....

News of the terrible explosion was relayed to Victoria, and just before midnight of the 24th, a special train carrying Robert Dunsmuir, doctors, and medical supplies was rushed from Russell's Station, on the outskirts of Victoria, to Wellington over the new Esquimalt and Nanaimo Railway. Accounts of the run vary, but it is believed that the Esquimalt and Nanaimo's No. 1, with engineer Aaron Garland at the throttle, covered the 77 mile distance in just over one and three quarters hours. As the train raced towards the present site of South Wellington, Robert Dunsmuir, alarmed by the high speed, told the conductor . . . "Conductor, you are running too fast, slow down a bit!" By the time conductor Weldon got up to the locomotive, the train had already reduced speed to pass through Nanaimo, five miles north of South Wellington.

The record-breaking speed was not the only feature making this run one to be remembered. Engine No. 1, a high-wheeled 4-4-0 had been fitted with a new pair of pilot wheels just a day before its hurried run to Wellington. When the locomotive returned to Russell's for inspection, it was discovered that a 14-inch long section of the flange on the right leading wheel was missing. It was located near Langford Lake, just north of Victoria. It was lying on the right hand side of the tracks, indicating that the train was travelling north when the wheel was chipped. The crews could hardly believe that the No. 1 had highballed all the way to Wellington with the broken flange. It was a miracle that the special relief train did not meet with disaster on the way.

After the mining accident, a list of the victims was published in the Department of Mines Annual Report for 1889. This list, in giving the sad results of the gas explosion in the No. 5 Mine, also revealed the differing status of the white and Chinese workers. While the whites were listed by their full names, the Chinese miners were listed by numbers assigned to them... "Chinaman No. 14, Bun; Chinaman No. 23, Gin; Chinaman No. 100, Sing Fom; . . . R. Robinson's Chinaman, No. 34, Jow; F. McCoy's Chinaman, No. 68, Jim; James Morrison's Chinaman, No. 76, Yon; Chinaman No. 78, Ton . . ." So anxious were the Chinese immigrants to find employment, that if one man left the mines because of sickness, injury, or death, his position was immediately taken by another, who assumed the former's name and number. Sometimes, white workers would hire Chinese themselves, paying them a low wage in return for the coal they produced. This made it possible for the white miner to claim a higher output of coal for his shift, substantially increasing his wage.

In 1889, the Dunsmuir family received a severe blow with the death of Robert Dunsmuir at the age of 64. Shortly before his death, Robert had commissioned builders to construct a castle for himself and his wife, Joan. The story is told that in 1850 he had promised this castle to his bride of two years to induce her to move to Vancouver Island. He kept his promise, but he did not live to see the completion of his dream. *Craigdarroch Castle,* as it was named, still stands in Victoria as

Craigdarroch Castle in Victoria was built by Robert Dunsmuir for his wife Joan. The Island's coal baron died before his palatial home was completed. The building is still a prominent and intriguing feature of Victoria's skyline. — Robert D. Turner

Nanaimo's No. 1 Mine was one of the largest on the Island producing nearly 20 million tons of coal in the 55 years prior to closure in 1938. — Provincial Archives

The Vancouver Coal Mining and Land Company's fourth locomotive, the *London*, switches a train of 14 six-ton mine cars under the mine tipple for loading sometime in the 1880's. Note the steep grade on the main line leading up to the mine. — PROVINCIAL ARCHIVES

In this scene from about 1900, four beautiful sailing vessels wait to load a cargo of coal at the New Vancouver Coal Mining and Land Company's Nanaimo wharves. Downgraded from the tea and silk trade, many fine ships ended their days carrying coal. — PROVINCIAL ARCHIVES

On May 3, 1887, the Vancouver Coal Mining and Land Company's No. 1 Mine at Nanaimo was rocked by fire and explosions. Several days passed before rescue teams could enter the tunnels in a vain attempt to save the 150 trapped miners. It was one of the worst disasters in Canadian mining history. This photograph shows one of the small 0-4-0 type locomotives outside the smoking mine as its crew awaits word of any survivors. — PROVINCIAL ARCHIVES

a monument to the coal baron and railroad builder, Robert Dunsmuir.

Throughout the 1880's, the Vancouver Coal Mining and Land Company at Nanaimo had maintained its position as the Dunsmuirs' chief competitor. In the years since it had built the first railroad on Vancouver Island, two more locomotives had been imported from England. The first of these, the *Nanaimo,* was another 0-4-0T, almost identical to the early *Pioneer.* It was built by the Manning Wardle Company of Leeds in 1874 and was placed in service on the company's railroad in 1877. The second machine was a heavier inside-connected 0-6-0T, known as the *London.* This locomotive, also a Manning Wardle product, began work on the railroad in 1884. The railway had been kept to a high standard, and was laid with 56-pound rail over its entire length. One hundred and fifty coal cars of six ton capacity provided adequate rolling stock to handle the production of the company's mines, at Esplanade, Chase River, and South Field.

Following promising exploratory work between Nanaimo and Wellington, the Vancouver Coal Mining and Land Company began the development of their Northfield Mine. On July 31, 1888, the miners hit coal at a depth of 425 feet. The shaft was sunk through three layers of hard bituminous coal, which proved to be an extension of the famous Wellington seam. The coal seam at this point averaged about four feet in thickness. A railway grade was laid out which crossed the tracks of the Esquimalt and Nanaimo Railway, just recently extended from Nanaimo to Wellington. However, before the crossing could be constructed, it was necessary to gain permission from James Dunsmuir, who was at that time managing the E&N. Dunsmuir, who was not about to aid a major competitor in establishing a new mine, refused permission. The New Vancouver Coal Mining and Land Company, as the firm was renamed, had hoped to use parts of the abandoned grade of the South Wellington Colliery Company's railroad to Departure Bay, but because of Dunsmuir's refusal was forced to reroute its grade completely in order to pass under the E&N. The rerouted railroad, five miles long, was opened in 1889 and remained in service until the Northfield Mine was closed some years later.

After their father's death, James and Alex Dunsmuir continued to operate the Wellington coal mines throughout the 1890's. In 1895, they acquired the holdings of the East Wellington Colliery which had ceased operations because it could not finance further working of the mines. The East Wellington Colliery Railway from the mines to Departure Bay was abandoned and an extension of the Dunsmuirs' Wellington Colliery Railway was laid to the new holdings.

Gradually, however, the Wellington coal seam was being worked out. By the mid-1890's, the most lucrative deposits were nearly exhausted and the mines were becoming increasingly expensive to operate. At this time, a large outcropping of coal had been discovered by a man named Hodgeson on the south slope of Mount Benson, about seven miles southwest of Nanaimo. The initial outcropping, ranging in thickness from nine to eleven feet, was first exposed by an uprooted tree. Since the coal was on the property of the Esquimalt and Nanaimo Railway, Hodgeson reported the finding to James Dunsmuir. Dunsmuir was elated with the new coal deposit and is reported to have paid Hodgeson a substantial sum in reward for his discovery. The coal, of excellent quality, proved to be an extension of the Wellington seam, mined by the Dunsmuirs for so many years. Exploratory work began in 1895 and continued throughout the following year.

The findings were promising. Two outcroppings were uncovered, revealing fine, hard coal, up to 15 feet in thickness. Encouraged by these discoveries, James Dunsmuir began to plan for the large scale development of the new mines under the auspices of his Union Colliery Company and the Esquimalt and Nanaimo Railway. Plans were formulated to build a standard gauge railroad from the site of the mines, originally called Wellington Extension and later simply Extension, across the Harewood Plains and the property of the New Vancouver Coal Mining and Land Company, to the E&N Railway and eventually Departure Bay. Dunsmuir had survey crews in the field, clearing the right-of-way through the holdings of the New Vancouver Coal Mining and Land Company, when he was presented with a court injunction to stop work. It is safe to guess that Dunsmuir regretted the day a decade earlier when he refused to allow this same company permission to cross his Esquimalt and Nanaimo Railway. Now the positions were reversed and it was Dunsmuir who found himself at a disadvantage. The dispute was taken to court, but the rulings were not in Dunsmuir's favour.

Faced with no alternative, and not wishing to delay the development of the mines any further, Dunsmuir decided to establish his shipping wharves at Oyster Harbour, a fine sheltered bay about 15 miles south of Nanaimo. Speed was important, since the closure of the old Wellington mines was iminent. A new spur line was built from the mines at Extension to a point on the E&N just north of the Nanaimo River. The new junction was named Fiddick's. This route utilized as much existing E&N trackage as possible and caused minimal delays in bringing the mines to production, as coal was already being stockpiled at the pitheads in preparation for shipment.

While work proceeded on the railway connection, coal bunkers and shipping facilities were constructed at Oyster Harbour. The bunkers were 400 feet long, 38 feet wide, and 25 feet deep, and were capable of holding approximately 8,000 tons of coal. Chutes were built on either side of the bunkers so that coal could be loaded into cars underneath on tracks leading to the shipping wharves. A dock for railway car barges was also constructed, making it possible to interchange freight cars and export coal directly by rail to the mainland of British Columbia. By the turn of the century, the Extension mines were in full production, yielding over 400,000 tons of coal annually.

As soon as the new rail connection was completed, passenger service was inaugurated between Ladysmith, as Dunsmuir named his new town on Oyster Harbour, and Extension. Timetables for the period show three round trips a day running between the two points. Dunsmuir hoped to have all the miners living away from the diggings at his planned community, but soon found it impossible to stop many workers from moving to Extension where a small town began to grow.

The new rail line was less than ideal, however. It was long and caused particularly heavy traffic concentration on the main line of the E&N. The dangers of this aspect of the operation was tragically reinforced in September 1901 when a disastrous head-on collision two miles north of Ladysmith resulted in the loss of four lives. Dunsmuir saw his only long-term answer to the transportation problem lying in the construction of a new railroad to Ladysmith, completely independent of the E&N. By 1901, grading of the new line was underway but work was not completed for several more years. The new railway route shortened the distance between the mines and the shipping wharves by about 2.5 miles and eliminated all use of the E&N by the colliery trains. A few years later, the E&N spur from Fiddick's Junction was abandoned except for a short section leading to one of the company's ballast pits.

While the mines at Extension were being brought to production, disaster struck on the Union Colliery Railway at Cumberland. On August 17, 1898, the company's newest locomotive, the No. 4, a big Baldwin Ten-Wheeler, pulled out of Cumberland with 21 loaded gondola cars, bound for the shipping wharves at Union Bay. The locomotive was carrying passengers in the cab that day, including two company workmen and two young women, in addition to the regular three man crew. Two Chinese miners were riding in one of the loaded cars just behind the locomotive. Nothing seemed out of the ordinary until the big Baldwin wheeled onto the 100-foot high trestle over the Trent River. Without warning, the bridge

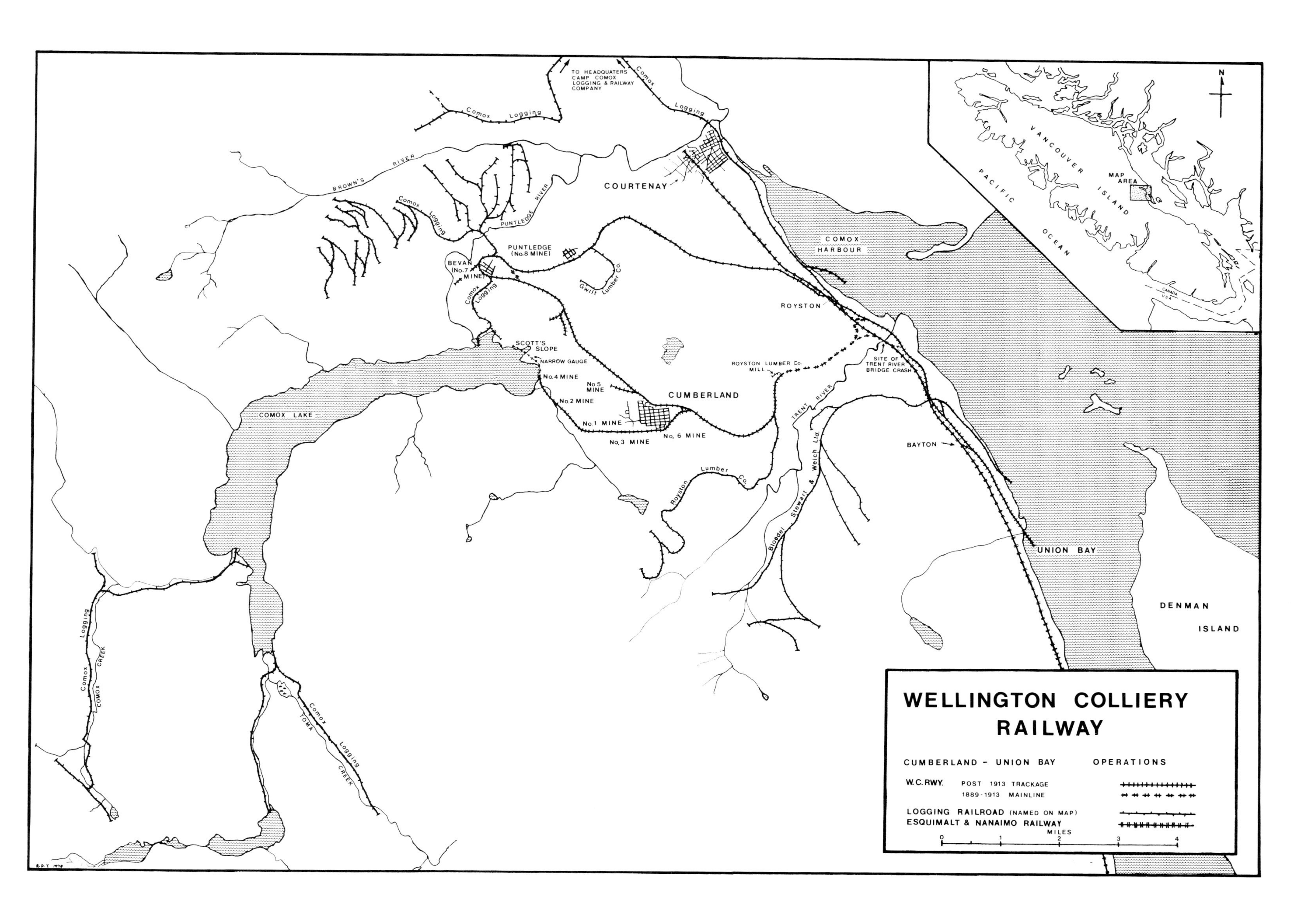
WELLINGTON COLLIERY RAILWAY
CUMBERLAND - UNION BAY OPERATIONS
W.C. RWY. POST 1913 TRACKAGE
1889-1913 MAINLINE
LOGGING RAILROAD (NAMED ON MAP)
ESQUIMALT & NANAIMO RAILWAY
MILES
0
1
2
3
4
N
VANCOUVER ISLAND
PACIFIC OCEAN
MAP AREA
CANADA
USA
TO HEADQUATERS CAMP COMOX LOGGING & RAILWAY COMPANY
Comox Logging
COURTENAY
BROWN'S RIVER
PUNTLEDGE RIVER
PUNTLEDGE (No.8 MINE)
BEVAN (No.7 MINE)
Gwilt Lumber Co.
COMOX HARBOUR
ROYSTON
SCOTT'S SLOPE
NARROW GAUGE
No.4 MINE
No.5 MINE
No.2 MINE
No.1 MINE
No.3 MINE
No. 6 MINE
CUMBERLAND
ROYSTON LUMBER Co. MILL
SITE OF TRENT RIVER BRIDGE CRASH
TRENT RIVER
Bloedel Stewart & Welch Ltd.
Royston Lumber Co.
BAYTON
UNION BAY
DENMAN ISLAND
COMOX LAKE
COMOX CREEK
TOMA CREEK

Union Colliery Railway's No. 4 plunged through the high wooden trestle over the Trent River on August 17, 1898. Seven people were killed and the train of 21 hopper cars was a total wreck. The scene on the left shows the trestle after the wreck, while (BELOW) a work crew examines the twisted remains of the locomotives. — BOTH PROVINCIAL ARCHIVES

collapsed under the train, sending the locomotive and cars plunging into the canyon below. Only two of those riding the train survived the crash. The fireman, Hugh Grant, and one of the women, a Miss Horne, escaped with serious injuries. The tragedy was one of the worst train wrecks ever to occur on Vancouver Island.

The wrecked locomotive was salvaged and rebuilt, and remained with the company until the end of railroad operations over 60 years later. The bridge over the Trent River was repaired, but was used only until the grade could be rerouted to a lower, safer crossing of the river nearer to Union Bay. Soon after the disaster passenger service was increased from the twice weekly mixed train between Cumberland and Union Bay, to a daily return service.

Locomotive No. 15 (formerly No. 5) was, with the exception of its slope-back tender, nearly identical to the No. 4 involved in the wreck pictured above. — JOHN LOCKNER

Between 1899 and 1901, the Dunsmuirs phased out their operations at Wellington, eventually abandoning the original railway to Departure Bay and all of the associated facilities. The town of Wellington was moved piece by piece to Ladysmith, where James was building a new town for the workers. The population of Wellington dropped from 5,000 in 1898 to only 100 three years later.

For some years, Alex Dunsmuir had been capably managing his company's interests in San Francisco at its office at 620 East Street. Alex had been anxious to purchase the shares of the company owned by his mother, Joan Dunsmuir, following the death of his father in 1889. This agreement was finally concluded on December 13, 1899, when James and Alex paid Mrs. Dunsmuir $400,000 for her colliery investments. Alex had purchased the old Souther Farm in Oakland, California, and had built a mansion in the tradition of his father's *Craigdarroch Castle* in Victoria. Alex's home still stands in Oakland today, and is known

James Dunsmuir, pictured on the left, succeeded his father Robert as head of the vast coal mining and railway interests controlled by the Dunsmuir family on Vancouver Island. — PROVINCIAL ARCHIVES (BELOW) For the visit to Cumberland of Baron Byng, Governor General of Canada, locomotive No. 20 was polished and decorated to pull the special train of Canadian Pacific equipment over the Wellington Colliery Railway. — JOHN LOCKNER

as *Dunsmuir House*. It was purchased by the City of Oakland for use as a research conference center. Alex, however, did not live long to enjoy his new home. Married on December 21, 1899, he died only 40 days later at age 46. He left all his property and assets to his older brother, James, who became the sole owner of the vast Dunsmuir colliery operations on Vancouver Island.

James had a peculiar relationship with his employees. Being brought up in the mines, and trained as a machinist, he was accepted by the men, and many of them knew him on a first name basis. He was popular and well respected because of his quiet and honest nature. However, he was also known as a dictatorial employer, who fought

Increased production at the Cumberland mines called for new and heavier power to handle the coal trains. As a result, 2-8-2 No. 20 was built for the Wellington Colliery Railway by the Baldwin Locomotive Works in 1913. Here the husky locomotive is seen about to leave Cumberland with a long train of loaded steel hopper cars. — W. JOHNSTONE COLLECTION

a continuing series of battles with the miners' unions, refusing to recognize them. Lockouts and strikes were frequent. Like his father, he entered public office and became Member of the Provincial Legislature for Comox, and eventually Premier of British Columbia between 1900 and 1902. Later, between 1906 and 1909, he served as Lieutenant Governor of the Province.

In 1905, Dunsmuir sold the Esquimalt and Nanaimo Railway and its vast land grant to the Canadian Pacific Railway Company. He retained coal rights to all of the lands, however, and continued to operate the Extension and Cumberland collieries until 1910. At this time, he sold his interests to MacKenzie and Mann of the Canadian Northern Railway for $7,000,000. They recapitalized the property and sold it to British interests, which formed Canadian Collieries (Dunsmuir) Limited to operate the mines. James retired to his estate near Victoria, called *Hatley Park*, or "Dunsmuir" Castle, until his death in 1920. *Hatley Park* is now part of the Canadian Services College at Royal Roads.

After the takeover of the Dunsmuir colliery interests by Canadian Collieries (Dunsmuir) Limited, the Cumberland and Extension railroads continued to be operated as the Wellington Colliery Railway. However, the company's locomotives and rolling stock were gradually relettered for Canadian Collieries (Dunsmuir) Ltd.

In 1912, a major relocation of the main line at Cumberland was undertaken following the opening of the No. 8 Mine at Puntledge. Previously, the tracks had extended as far as Bevan, near Comox Lake, where trains were turned and run back through Cumberland to Union Bay. The new route, while more indirect than the old line, eliminated the grade following the Trent River. It curved in an easterly direction from Puntledge to Royston on Comox Harbour, where it connected with the Comox Logging and Railway Company's line. From there it ran in a southeasterly direction to rejoin the old line to Union Bay at a point just north of the Trent River. The new line was laid with 80-pound rail and had a maximum grade of two percent.

With traffic on the increase, it soon became apparent that a new locomotive was needed at Union Bay. As a result, in 1913, the first and only new locomotive acquired by Dunsmuir's successors was placed in service on the heavy coal trains. The

Form R 300

WELLINGTON COLLIERY RAILWAY COMPANY

FOR THE INFORMATION AND GOVERNMENT OF EMPLOYEES ONLY

CUMBERLAND DIVISION

TIME TABLE NO. 10

TAKING EFFECT 12.01 A.M., SUNDAY, JULY 7TH, 1929

PACIFIC STANDARD TIME

NORTH BOUND TRAIN Inferior Direction MIXED 1 ARRIVE Mon., Tues. Weds., Thurs. Friday, Sat.	Distance From Cumberland	STATIONS	Distance From Union Bay	SOUTH BOUND TRAIN Superior Direction MIXED 2 LEAVE Mon., Tues. Weds., Thurs. Friday, Sat.
4.40	.0	Ar. CUMBERLAND Lv.	18.8	9.00
	1.0	Y Phone	17.8	
4.25	5.6	BEVAN	13.2	9.30
4.20	7.9	PUNTLEDGE	10.9	9.40
4.15	9.3	LAKE TRAIL ROAD	9.5	9.42
4.10	10.4	COURTENAY ROAD	8.4	9.45
4.05	11.5	MINTO ROAD	7.3	9.48
4.00	13.5	ROYSTON	5.3	9.55
	18.8	Lv. UNION BAY Phone Ar.	.0	

SOUTH BOUND TRAINS ARE SUPERIOR TO NORTH BOUND TRAINS OF THE SAME CLASS

SPECIAL RULES

1. All previous time tables must be destroyed.
2. Registering Stations: Cumberland and Union Bay
3. Bulletin Stations: " " "
4. Official Clock: " " "
5. E. & N. Ry. Diamond Crossing at Royston, mileage 13.5, is governed by interlocking rules; all trains must be under control for signals at this crossing.
6. The Company's rules are printed separately in book form. Every employee whose duties are connected with the movement of trains must have a copy of the rules and the current time table accessible when on duty.

WELLINGTON COLLIERY RAILWAY COMPANY

Employees timetable for July 7, 1929 showed only two scheduled trains on the Cumberland to Union Bay line of the Wellington Colliery Railway. Soon after, all passenger service was abandoned on the railroad. — JOHN HOFFMEISTER COLLECTION

locomotive was a large, low-drivered Baldwin 2-8-2 and was the heaviest engine ever to operate on the mining railroads on Vancouver Island. The big machine remained on the company's roster as the No. 20 for 45 years before being scrapped in March 1958. Peak periods at the Cumberland mines saw trains operating 24 hours a day, with three locomotives working in the yards while another three handled tonnage on the main line.

In 1914, an extension of the Esquimalt and Nanaimo Railway was built to Courtenay, 9.5 miles north of Union Bay. Interchange tracks were established at Royston, providing a new outlet for coal and coke. In addition, the Wellington Colliery Railway provided a connecting passenger service with the E&N resulting in an increase in travel over the line. Regular service between Union Bay and Cumberland remained in effect until 1930, when declining patronage and a worsening economic climate forced its abandonment.

In addition to the standard gauge railroad operations between Union Bay, Cumberland and the mines, a small 3-foot gauge line was maintained to connect the workings at Scott's Slope, on the east-

The locomotive *San Francisco* was purchased new from Baldwin in 1896 for operation at the Nanaimo colliery. — NANAIMO MUSEUM (RIGHT) In later years the *San Francisco*, then simply No. 5, and the identical No. 6 shown in the photograph were modified by the addition of larger enclosed cabs and small tenders. — ALBERT H. PAULL

ern shore of Comox Lake, with the No. 4 Mine one mile to the south. Locomotive No. 19 (formerly *Victoria*) was used to haul coal to the No. 4 Mine for screening. Usually the trains consisted of the small tank locomotive and about 30 mine cars. This was not the only narrow gauge railway run by Canadian Collieries (Dunsmuir) Limited.

In addition to the railroads operated around the coal mines, extensive networks of narrow gauge tracks were laid in the mine tunnels below the surface. These were used for moving men, equipment, and coal between the pit heads and tipples and the workings hundreds of feet below. The underground rail operations were complex and varied. In the early days, cars were moved by hand or pulled by mules. Steam hauling engines were also used to winch the cars up the incline shafts to the surface. In later years, in some of the larger mines, such as the Nos. 1, 2, 3, and 6 Mines at Extension, electric locomotives were used to move the coal cars. In this operation, the entire output of the Nos. 1, 2, and 3 Mines was brought to the tipple by rail through a double tracked,

By 1930 when No. 7 was photographed at Nanaimo, the mines in the area had come under the control of Canadian Collieries (Dunsmuir) Ltd. No. 7, which is also shown on page 22 in the photo of the No. 1 Mine, was originally tenderless. Later it was modified to pull a four-wheeled tender as seen on No. 6. Finally, both No. 7 and No. 8 were equipped with the style shown here. — ALBERT H. PAULL

No. 9 was the only 4-6-0 operated at the Nanaimo mines. It was acquired secondhand from the Grand Trunk Pacific to replace the old *London*. It ended its days providing steam to pump out one of the mines at Reserve, south of Nanaimo. — Albert H. Paull

heavily timbered 7 by 14-foot rock tunnel, built on a one percent grade meeting the No. 1 Mine about three quarters of a mile from the surface. It also ran about one-half mile into the No. 3 Mine and another one and a quarter miles into the No. 2 Mine. Employees were taken to and from the workings in "man trips," hauled by Baldwin-Westinghouse electric locomotives operated from an overhead trolley system. Coal was hauled by similar methods, with loaded trains frequently reaching 100 cars in length. In addition to this operation, the No. 6 Mine was connected to the tipple at Extension by a one mile long narrow gauge surface railway and a 3,000-foot incline.

While Canadian Collieries (Dunsmuir) Limited was prospering, so too was its chief competitor, the Western Fuel Corporation of Canada, the successor to the New Vancouver Coal Mining and Land Company. By the 1920's, all of the original British tank locomotives had been disposed of. All traffic was handled by four large Baldwin 0-6-0 tank locomotives equipped with tenders and an old 4-6-0 of Pittsburgh and Lake Erie origin which the company had acquired from the Grand Trunk Pacific to replace the British built *London* when it was scrapped in 1918. Rolling stock had been regularly upgraded, and by the mid-1920's, the company was operating two passenger cars, 42 flat cars, 21 work cars, and 564 coal cars of various types over its 20-mile railroad. In 1928, the entire operation was purchased by Canadian Collieries (Dunsmuir) Limited for $1,730,000, giving Canadian Collieries a virtual monopoly over the Vancouver Island coal fields.

Two minor competitors of Canadian Collieries (Dunsmuir) Limited should also be noted. In 1913, Pacific Coast Coal Mines Limited opened the Morden Mine and two other shafts at South Wellington. A standard gauge railroad was built to a terminal at Boat Harbour, south of Nanaimo. Three small locomotives were operated over the route until 1921, when the mines were closed. In the 1920's, another small mining operation was opened. The King and Foster Coal Company worked over the areas mined by the Dunsmuirs at Wellington in the 1800's. It recovered the outcrop pillars left from the original mining operations and employed two small locomotives and about ten cars to move the salvaged coal over its one and a quarter mile long railway.

Locomotive No. 11 was typical of four 2-4-2 type tank engines acquired by the Wellington Colliery Railway. Initially, the engines operated primarily on the Extension to Ladysmith line but in later years they also worked at Nanaimo. — Provincial Archives (BELOW) Baldwin 4-6-0 No. 15 and the very similar Nos. 10 and 14 were used in main line service at both Extension and Cumberland. On occasion they could even be seen working on the Esquimalt and Nanaimo. — R. J. Knight

The general economic depression following the great "crash" of 1929 resulted in a rapid decrease in the worldwide demand for coal. Faced with reduced sales in the established markets and the increasing competition from oil producers, the colliery companies slowed down work in all of the mines. In some cases, the closure of the older workings was hastened, as the costs of keeping the shafts dewatered and in repair could not be justified by the quantities of coal remaining in the diggings. On April 10, 1931, the whole of the Extension Colliery was closed down and permanently abandoned. By the time of the closure, over 8,000,000 tons of coal had been produced from the rich seams. The railroad was abandoned between Ladysmith and Extension shortly after, and the docks and other facilities were soon torn down. However, the large steel bridge over the Nanaimo River was left intact and was used by the Comox Logging and Railway Company when it began logging in the Nanaimo Lakes region in 1943.

The extension of logging operations along the Nanaimo River facilitated the development of one of the last mines to open in the Ladysmith area. In 1943 diamond drilling along the Nanaimo River west of Extension revealed a limited but workable coal deposit at a site named White Rapids. There a mine was developed by Canadian Collieries (Dunsmuir) Limited. It is highly unlikely that by itself, the output of this small mine would have justified the reconstruction of the Wellington Colliery Railway. However, because it was possible to utilize the new logging railway, the operation became economically feasible. The coal was shipped over the Comox Logging and Railway Company's line to the E&N Railway at Storms, where in 1944 an interchange track was built. Shipments from White Rapids, which averaged about six carloads of coal a day, were then delivered by the E&N to the colliery company at Stockett Junction for movement to the coal washing plant and shipping wharves on the Nanaimo waterfront. The White Rapids Mine continued in production until July 1950, when the workings were abandoned.

Coal produced in the same area by Canadian Collieries (Dunsmuir) Limited at its No. 5, 10 and Alexandria Mines at South Wellington was all shipped over the E&N to the loading facilities at Ladysmith or, after 1930, to Nanaimo. Some coal was also exported in carload shipments using the

Coal passes through the tipple of the Bright Mine at Nanaimo. — Provincial Archives (ABOVE RIGHT) Reliable No. 14 pulls a six car miners' train into Ladysmith from Extension. During peak periods of production similar trains carried hundreds of miners to and from the workings each day. — R. J. Knight Collection (RIGHT) Locomotive No. 17, one of the last operational mining engines on the Island sits outside the Union Bay shops just a few years before being sold for preservation in Washington. — Dave Wilkie

railway car ferry at Ladysmith. The last of these mines, the No. 10, was closed down in 1951, leaving only the Bright Mine at Cassidy in operation. Coal from this mine was hauled by truck to Nanaimo.

By the mid-1930's, Wellington Colliery Railway locomotives had replaced all but two of the former Western Fuel Corporation's engines at Nanaimo. The roster of the Wellington Colliery Railway itself had been substantially reduced by this time and most of the older machines had been disposed of. The railroads at Nanaimo remained in operation until 1950, when all of the remaining equipment was scrapped or moved north to the mines at Union Bay. All large scale mining in the area ceased in November 1953, when the Bright Mine was closed.

At Union Bay, colliery trains continued to operate from Cumberland over the main line to the docks into the early 1950's. Business was augmented by hauling a good deal of timber for the Comox Logging and Railway Company, whose line connected with the Canadian Colliery operation at Bevan. In addition, much of the export from the large mill of the Royston Lumber Company, just east of Cumberland, was moved over the colliery railroad to the interchange with the Esquimalt and Nanaimo Railway at Royston.

In 1953, the No. 8 Mine was closed down and the main line of Canadian Collieries (Dunsmuir) Limited's railway was abandoned north of Bayton. Here, a new interchange track to the Esquimalt and Nanaimo Railway was constructed. Switching operations continued at Union Bay, to handle coal trucked in from the Tsable Mine, south of Union Bay. This mine was finally closed down in 1960, and the last section of the Wellington Colliery Railway was abandoned in August of that year. Only two locomotives remained on the property: the No. 17, a saddle tanker equipped with a tender, and the No. 14, the former Union Colliery Railway No. 4 which had crashed through the Trent River Bridge 62 years before. Both of these machines were purchased by the Puget Sound

Canadian Collieries (Dunsmuir) Ltd.'s No. 4 Mine at Cumberland was a major source of traffic for the railroad to Union Bay. — W. Johnstone Collection

The four-masted *Pamir*, shown on the left, was the last of a generation of sailing vessels that hauled coal from the Vancouver Island mines to ports all over the world. Here, she is loading at Union Bay in 1946, bound for Australia. In the early 1950's, the *Pamir* went down with all hands in the North Atlantic. (ABOVE) The machine shops at Union Bay were capable of handling all types of locomotive repairs. — BOTH W. JOHNSTONE COLLECTION (BELOW) In August 1960, after 60 years of continuous service, the No. 14 switched the last carloads of coal from the Cumberland mines. — DAVE WILKIE

The Lenora, Mt. Sicker Railway was a turn of the century copper hauler that operated between the town of Crofton and the copper diggings on Mt. Sicker. This photograph shows Shay locomotive No. 1 loading ore at the mine bunkers. — PROVINCIAL ARCHIVES

Railway Historical Society and moved to Snoqualmie Falls for permanent preservation. Within a few years, the deep sea wharves and company buildings at Union Bay had been dismantled, and only a few bridges, level crossings, and sections of grade remained to show the route of the once busy railroad, and so ended the saga of the coal mining railroads of Vancouver Island.

Another interesting mining railroad on southern Vancouver Island was the Lenora Mt. Sicker Railway, which operated in the Crofton District around the turn of the century. In 1895, copper ore was discovered on the slopes of Mt. Sicker. Several claims were staked in the area, but it was not until two years later, when the Lenora claim was staked, that development of the copper deposits began. By January 1900, the Lenora Mine had reached production. Ore was hauled by wagon from Mt. Sicker down a steep grade to a siding on the Esquimalt and Nanaimo Railway. From there, it was transported to Ladysmith for shipment to a small smelter on Texada Island. At this time, the Lenora claim was purchased by a group headed by Henry Croft, who, incidentally, was married to one of Robert Dunsmuir's daughters. Croft and his associates soon found that the wagons could

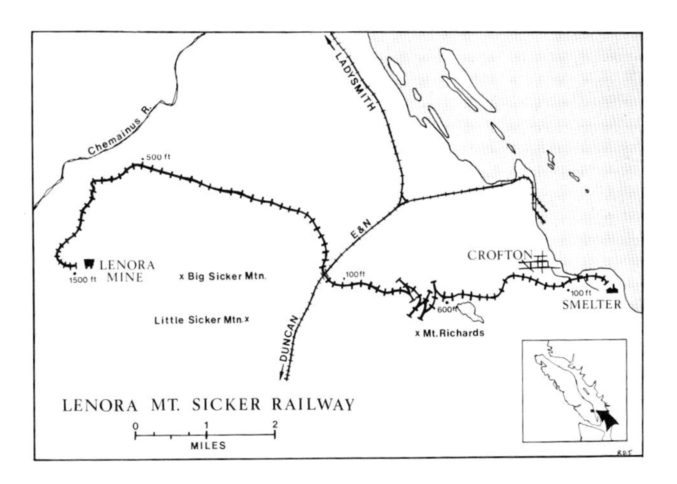

not move enough ore to keep up with production. To speed up the operation, they contracted to have a tramway built down to the E&N's Mt. Sicker siding.

The new tramway, while an improvement over the wagons, was still inadequate to handle the volume of ore being mined. In August 1900, construction work commenced on a short narrow gauge railroad from the mine directly to Osborn Bay, near the present site of Crofton. A. J. McLellan, a contractor who had built sections of the Esquimalt and Nanaimo Railway, was hired to undertake the construction work. A small geared locomotive, a Shay, was ordered from the Lima Locomotive Works and delivered by December. Initially, the railroad was constructed only as far as the Mt. Sicker siding, and ore was transferred for shipment north as before. The little Lenora No. 1 could handle one or two cars at a time on the grade, which for nearly a mile, climbed at a steep 13 percent. To keep up with production, a second slightly larger Shay locomotive was purchased second hand the following year.

In 1902, the last section of the eleven mile long railway, from the Mt. Sicker siding to Osborn Bay, was completed. Soon after, a third Shay, newly

Tiny Lenora No. 1 was one of the smallest Shay locomotives ever to operate on Vancouver Island. She weighed under 10 tons fully loaded and carried 6 x 10-inch cylinders. Lima built the machine in 1900. Here, No. 1 dumps a load of ore at Esquimalt and Nanaimo Railway's Mt. Sicker siding in 1901. The railway to Crofton had not yet been built. — PROVINCIAL ARCHIVES

Shay No. 3, built in 1902, was the newest and heaviest locomotive on the narrow gauge Lenora Mt. Sicker Railway. — PROVINCIAL ARCHIVES

built, was acquired from Lima to work on the steep grade between the mines and Mt. Sicker siding. A smelter was built at Crofton to process the ore. In addition, a barge slip with standard gauge trackage was constructed so that freight cars carrying shipments for the smelter could be unloaded directly at their destination. A small Forney locomotive was purchased for switching in the smelter yard. This machine had originally operated on the New York Elevated Railway. The little railway also provided a limited passenger service, carrying visitors and miners from the mine townsite at Mt. Sicker to the Mt. Sicker siding, where connection was made with the E&N's daily passenger trains. However, passenger traffic was very light, and in 1903, only 725 persons rode the little train.

Unfortunately, the prosperity enjoyed by the Lenora Mine was short lived. Legal disputes forced the company into receivership in 1904. The mine operated for a short time in 1905, but closed down the following year. It was reactivated briefly in 1907, only to be closed again. In 1908, the equipment was sold to various logging firms operating on the British Columbia coast, and soon after, the railway itself was dismantled.

In this view, No. 1 is seen working up the 13 percent grade on Haggerty Hill. This steep incline was a test for even the climbing abilities of a Shay locomotive. (BELOW) Lenora No. 1 was sold after the closure of the railway and operated for a number of owners on the coast. Here, the locomotive shows the effects of years of hard service, as the crew pause to be photographed at the Surrey Shingle Co. Ltd. at Sullivan (West Surrey), B. C. — Both Provincial Archives

Thundering upgrade on the spectacular wooden trestle over Niagara Canyon, one of the Esquimalt and Nanaimo Railway's 4-6-0's wheels a train of early vintage cars from Victoria over the Malahat to Nanaimo. — PROVINCIAL ARCHIVES

2

ESQUIMALT AND NANAIMO RAILWAY

IN 1871, when British Columbia joined the Confederation and became a Province of Canada, agreement was made to connect British Columbia with the Eastern provinces by a transcontinental railroad. John A. Macdonald, Prime Minister of Canada and driving force behind the "Pacific Railroad," promised that construction would begin in 1873. The immenseness of the task was staggering. By the summer of 1873, surveys and explorations were only beginning to present a picture of the alternate routes available through the rugged interior and coastal mountains to the coast of British Columbia. Construction engineers would only speculate which of several routes might ultimately provide the best right-of-way for the new railroad.

Feeling that he must take some action to demonstrate minimal progress on the railroad, Macdonald named the western terminus of the transcontinental line. It was to be Esquimalt, at the southern tip of Vancouver Island. At this time, the settlement was an important base for the Royal Navy, and was located only a few miles from the City of Victoria, the largest and most politically sensitive community on the west coast of Canada. Macdonald's declaration implied that the railway was to be routed from Esquimalt to the northern end of Vancouver Island, crossing to the mainland via Seymour Narrows and the northern islands of the Straits of Georgia to the shore of Bute Inlet. Residents of Vancouver Island were overjoyed.

Survey reports on this route were discouraging, however. The impracticability of building a direct rail connection between Vancouver Island and the mainland of British Columbia was clearly shown in the survey reports of the Canadian Pacific Railway's Marcus Smith:

> From the head of Bute Inlet, the line follows its western shore 50 miles down to the Arran rapids, which separate Stewart Island from the mainland. The whole of this on the rocky slopes of high mountains, very irregular and broken; . . . With undulating grades, and curves as sharp as 900 feet radius, the work on this portion will be excessively heavy; there will be a large quantity of rock excavation . . . and a great number of tunnels from 100 to 3,000 feet in length, amounting in the aggregate to eight miles . . .
>
> From this point on the mainland to the west shore of the Seymour Narrows the line crosses by Stewart, Valdes (now called Quadra) and Maude Islands, in a rather circuitous course, to avoid high rocky hills. The distance is about 29 miles and there are six intervening channels of great depth, through which the tide flows at the rate of four to nine knots. The rock excavation in crossing these islands will be heavy, with a few short tunnels; altogether the works on this section will be of a most formidable character.

In total, six spans ranging in length from 1,100 to 1,350 feet and one span of 640 feet would have been required to bridge the channels. The cost of the line would have been staggering. Even if steam ferries were used to make the crossing, the cost of bringing the line to Esquimalt would have been about $20,000,000 more than the expenditure required to reach Burrard Inlet on the mainland.

On Vancouver Island itself, few serious problems appeared except in finding a right-of-way around the Malahat Range north of Esquimalt. Even though a coastal route was chosen, rock work would be heavy. Lines were also surveyed to Alberni and Quatsino Sound where it was felt port facilities might be developed.

Speculation and hope continued that the railroad would be brought directly to Vancouver Island. Residents of Vancouver Island still considered the construction of a rail line between Esquimalt and Nanaimo an immediate necessity even if the more ambitious schemes had to be delayed. Islanders grew increasingly impatient over the lack of progress on the railroad. In order to quiet the situation, a sod-turning ceremony was held at Esquimalt and a short section of line was cleared during July 1873. However, after this action, work on the railroad ceased and the islanders and British Columbians in general became indignant over the delay. Protests and delegations were sent to the Federal Government and even to Queen Victoria. Secession was threatened unless construction of the promised railroad was started immediately. An arbitrator, Lord Carnarvon, was appointed and British Columbia and the Federal Government, now under Alexander Mackenzie, agreed to abide by the terms of his settlement. Carnarvon ordered an extension in the construction time of the transcontinental railroad and maintained that the section of line on Vancouver Island between Esquimalt and Nanaimo be an integral part of the system.

Early in 1875, Mackenzie had a bill introduced into Parliament to undertake construction of the Vancouver Island line. Although it passed the House of Commons by a narrow margin, it was defeated in the Senate. Long negotiations and more discussion of separation followed. An Order-in-Council was then issued, offering British Columbia $750,000 cash instead of the Island Railway, but the proposal was rejected by British Columbia. The Mackenzie government eventually stated that the railroad on Vancouver Island was not to be considered a part of the main line of the transcontinental railway, and therefore should be basically a local undertaking.

In a federal election held in 1878, the Mackenzie government was defeated and John A. Macdonald's government was returned to power, although Macdonald himself was defeated in his own Kingston, Ontario, district. He was re-elected in a by-election held in Victoria. As a Member of Parliament from Victoria, as well as Prime Minister, he had an added incentive for pushing ahead with construction of the transcontinental railway and the line on Vancouver Island. More delays and negotiations followed the election, but finally on October 4, 1879, an Order-in-Council was issued designating the shore of Burrard Inlet, the present site of Vancouver, as the new western terminus of the transcontinental railway. Construction soon began on the first section of right-of-way between Yale in the Fraser Canyon and Savona's Ferry, west of Kamloops. Vancouver Islanders were still frustrated by the continued delay in building the long desired line from Esquimalt to Nanaimo.

In 1881, Amor de Cosmos, Premier of British Columbia, tried to persuade the syndicate in control of the Canadian Pacific Railway to undertake the building of the Vancouver Island railway, but was not successful. The following year, two groups petitioned the Provincial Legislature for the right to build the railway. One of these groups, headed by Lewis M. Clements, was granted a charter under the name, "Vancouver Land and Railway Company." It was to build the railway from Esquimalt to Seymour Narrows in return for nearly 2,000,000 acres of land — in a 20-mile wide strip running north from Goldstream to Seymour Narrows. A second group headed by Robert and James Dunsmuir, the famed colliery operators, had unsuccessfully applied for a charter for the construction of the "Victoria, Esquimalt and Nanaimo Railway."

Clements' group could not raise sufficient capital to begin work, however, and the proposal fell through. Further negotiations took place between the Provincial and Federal Governments, and it was finally agreed that the Dunsmuirs and their associates should undertake to build a railway on the Island between Esquimalt and Nanaimo, in return for the Vancouver Island Land Grant, previously offered to Clements' group. In addition, they would receive $750,000 from the Federal Government as a direct subsidy. To secure these arrangements, the Province was obliged to turn over 3,500,000 acres of land in the Peace River district of northern British Columbia to the Federal Government to compensate for federal lands given to the railway builders.

On August 20, 1883, a provisional contract had been agreed upon and signed by Robert and James Dunsmuir, along with John Bryden, also of Vancouver Island, Charles Crocker and Leland Stanford, of San Francisco, and Collis P. Huntington of New York. The last three were well known railroad giants of the Central Pacific Railroad, and with their backing, the Dunsmuirs were assured of success in their new venture.

The railroad was incorporated on September 27, 1883. The terms of the act stipulated that the railroad was to be completed within three years. By late April in 1884, the actual construction of the Esquimalt and Nanaimo Railway, as it was called, had commenced. Dunsmuir selected as his chief engineer the highly competent and experienced Joseph Hunter. Hunter had previously worked for the Canadian Pacific Railway on location surveys on the west coast. He had explored the route now followed by the British Columbia Railway (formerly the Pacific Great Eastern) from Squamish through to the Lillooet River. He had also surveyed and explored large parts of the interior of British Columbia and had been commissioned to locate passes over the Cascade Mountains. He had worked on Vancouver Island as a Federal Government surveyor of a section of right-of-way between Nanaimo and Mill Bay when the transcontinental railway was first being planned.

On April 30, 1884, Dunsmuir issued orders for the construction work to begin. He dispatched the following brief but explicit note to Joseph Hunter:

Victoria, 30th April, 1884

Joseph Hunter, Esq.,

Dear Sir:

As engineer in chief you will at once proceed with the location of the line between Esquimalt and Nanaimo in accordance with the agreement entered into between the Dominion Government and the Esquimalt and Nanaimo Railway Company, of which company I am president.

You will be expected to locate the line with the view to the least expenditure in construction consistent with good work and to carry on the work to completion without delay. You will be responsible for all expenditure in your department, returning proper vouchers duly signed to this office and report to me your progress in the work as often as possible.

Yours truly,

Robert Dunsmuir, President.

Hunter devoted the next five months to survey work and to preparing for awarding the contracts for construction. The route he chose, or, in some cases, was forced to accept, was rugged and was judged by some to be impractical. The first section of the route, from Esquimalt through the rolling coastal lowlands to Goldstream followed an easy grade, but from there, in the ascent of the rocky Malahat Range, the grade stiffened to 1.74 percent. The line wound along sheer cliffs 800 to 900 feet above the deep waters of glacier scoured Finlayson Arm and traversed several deep canyons. At the Malahat summit, the grade leveled off, descending gradually past Shawnigan Lake and across the Cowichan River to "Duncan's." From there to Nanaimo, 33 miles away, an easy route was traced through the still densely forested coastal lowlands which extend from the Cowichan River to Campbell River.

The first tenders to be called, in September 1884, were for construction of 25 miles of the subgrade between Nanaimo and the Chemainus River. The $200,000 contract was awarded to Messrs. Graham and Bush, who proceeded immediately with the clearing of the right-of-way. In February of the following year, a contract for the construction of the first 22 miles of right-of-way north from Esquimalt was awarded to A. J. McLellan. This section extended over the Malahat to Cliffside, near Shawnigan Lake.

The Victoria and Nanaimo newspapers of 1884 and 1885 were full of news of the long delayed railroad. On May 19, 1885, the *Daily Colonist* ran the following report of the construction work north of Victoria:

The rapid progress of the McLellan Contract of the Island railway is very apparent even to a superficial observer while driving from Victoria to Goldstream. The first point where one meets the road is shortly after leaving Craigflower Bridge, where gangs of men are at work blasting and grading. Just before reaching Parson's Bridge a large number of white men are at work constructing trestle work for a long fill to meet the grade at the opposite side of the wagon road. The camps of the workmen are scattered all along the road until Goldstream is reached.

The first four locomotives on the Esquimalt and Nanaimo Railway were high-drivered 4-4-0's or American Standards of classic proportions. They were built by the Schenectady Locomotive Works between 1884 and 1886, had 17 x 24-inch cylinders and 64-inch drivers. In the scene above, No. 1 has just arrived at Russell's Station and is being inspected by the shop crew and members of the office staff. — PROVINCIAL ARCHIVES

The railway will cross about 150 feet below the romantic fall of water. Grading on either side of the stream is completed and the bridge crossing the deep ravine will soon be erected. At the west side of the stream, Mr. Antonelli's contract begins (*note*: rock work was sub-contracted to Antonelli by McLellan), extending for a distance of five miles. This is principally rock work, the hardest piece on the whole McLellan contract. Already one mile of the grade is completed for the ties and rails. About one hundred whites and 250 Chinese are engaged on this subcontract. There are several extensive rock cuttings and very deep fill, and a tunnel of 200 feet (actually 145 feet) on this five mile stretch. It is expected that the rails will be laid beyond Goldstream and the construction train running to that point by about the first week in September.

Meanwhile, contracts had been awarded to Messrs. Bell, Larkin, and Paterson to lay the tracks on the northern portion of the line from Nanaimo to the end of the McLellan construction work at Cliffside. In July 1885, rail and construction equipment began to arrive on Vancouver Island. Shipments of rail were brought into Esquimalt aboard the *Nagpore* and into Oyster Harbour (now the site of Ladysmith) aboard the *Barnard Castle*. Later that month, the steamer *Wellington* entered Oyster Harbour with the first locomotive, the No. 1, for the new Esquimalt and Nanaimo Railway. The arrival of this engine, a modern Schenectady built 4-4-0, was reported with enthusiasm in the *Nanaimo Free Press* of July 25th:

> The Pioneer Locomotive of the Island Railway was safely landed on the track. Captain Young, with coat off saying "come on" to his willing officers and men and the machinery available on the steamer, combined with the excellent arrangements which had been provided on shore under the personal direction of Mr. Dunsmuir speedily accomplished without hitch, what was by no means an inconsiderable undertaking. The discharge of a ponderous locomotive of 40 tons weight in one piece at an out of the way "port" like Oyster Harbour. Rails are being laid on the siding and there will soon be a busy time.

Under the direction of Aaron Garland, the company's first locomotive engineer, the machine was placed in service early in August. With a locomo-

The impressive curved trestle over the Double Head Ravine is no longer a part of the E&N's scenic climb over the Malahat between Victoria and Duncan. Shown here soon after completion in 1885, it was filled in during 1907 because of high maintenance costs. (BELOW) Brand new and on one of its first runs over the E&N is locomotive No. 2. The photograph was taken at Goldstream, an area that is now a Provincial Park. — BOTH PROVINCIAL ARCHIVES

tive available, it was possible to step up the pace of construction work. Track was laid from Chemainus north to the Nanaimo River, where it was necessary to construct a major bridge. The Howe truss bridges, used for this crossing and that of the Chemainus River, were framed at Chemainus and transported over the railway to the bridge sites.

On August 12, 1885, E&N's No. 2, the *Victoria*, and a number of flatcars arrived at Esquimalt aboard the *Wellington*. They were to be used for construction work on the southern portion of the line. By this time, grading was proceeding rapidly toward the Malahat summit. All rock work on the east of the tunnel was finished, and 20 feet of the 145-foot tunnel had been bored, with completion of the remaining section scheduled for the beginning of October.

On the 1st of October, the *Daily Colonist* made the following report on the Nanaimo section of the line:

> The Bell, Larkin, and Paterson contract of the Island railway is progressing very favourably. Twenty miles of track is laid and the ballast train is now busy. The Nanaimo River bridge was completed on Monday and the iron horse will soon be seen at Nanaimo Station. It is also expected that the Chemainus River bridge will be finished in a few days and track laying commenced to the Cowichan River, where piles are now being driven for the bridge. The road is ready for the rails to this point, and when laid, 35 miles from Nanaimo or half the distance between the city and Victoria will have been completed.

Construction work did not proceed without incident, however. On one occasion, bents for a 1,000-foot bridge were being assembled on the beach at Oyster Harbour when strong winds, coupled with a particularly high tide, carried the whole assembly out to sea! One hundred thousand feet of timber was lost.

Another incident was recalled by the late W. E. Losee for the *Daily Colonist* in 1932:

> It was during the construction of the big trestle over the Arbutus Canyon. There was a Swede working on the gang who was known as 'Swaybrace' Charlie, because he could pack a three by ten inch thirty foot swaybrace unaided. He was working on the deck of the trestle when he was struck by the trolley cable and was knocked off. He fell and lodged headfirst between a swaybrace and halter post fifty feet below. It took nearly an hour to get him free, and more time to lower him another fifty feet to the ground. His collar bone and shoulder blades were crushed, but he walked two miles over a horse trail to the Goldstream Hotel and then made the trip to Victoria by buggy. He recovered and was back at heavy work in due time.

On another occasion, a man by the name of Riley, acting as paymaster for the construction crews between Chemainus and Oyster Harbour, was robbed by a masked bandit just past Chemainus. The paymaster handed over the money without question and hurried back to the construction camp. The workmen immediately set out in search of the highwayman, but no clues to his whereabouts could be uncovered. After several weeks, hope of recovering the money had almost been given up, when the bandit was apprehended near Maple Bay with the stolen $14,000 by Con-

E&N No. 3 was delivered to the railway in 1885 and is shown here the following year at Russell's Station. This was the first terminal for the railway in the Victoria area and served all passenger trains until the tracks were extended across Victoria's Inner Harbour to a more convenient site in 1888. Note the snowplow attached to the locomotive's pilot. — PROVINCIAL ARCHIVES

stable Hall of the British Columbia Provincial Police Force. The crews received their wages, and the bandit was sentenced to five years in jail.

Aside from incidents such as these, there were the inevitable disputes over working conditions and wages. There was also considerable debate over the hiring of Chinese laborers for construction work.

By mid-August 1886, the line was nearly finished, with only ballasting to be completed. At Cliffside, where the construction crews met, the last spike was driven by Sir John A. Macdonald, Prime Minister of Canada, on August 13, at 10:00 A.M. "This was the junction of the McLellan and Earl and the Bell, Larkin, and Paterson contracts," reported the *Daily Colonist.* "Mr. McLellan, who was onboard, informed Sir John that in ten days his men had laid 20,000 ties and eight miles of track, besides preparing and erecting ten trestles which required 350,000 feet of timber. The Prime Minister expressed astonishment at the rapidity of the work and the solidity of track, which in his opinion, will rank with most of the railways in Eastern Canada. The party by this time had debarked and as the last rail was placed Sir John, armed with a silver mallet, advanced and drove the golden spike home as the last blow was delivered the ECHOES WERE DISTURBED for the first time since Creation with hearty cheers for Sir John and Lady Macdonald, Mr. Dunsmuir and the Island Railway."

Regular passenger service was inaugurated over the E&N with a special four car excursion train on September 24, 1886. Revenue service commenced on September 30, with trains departing Russell's Station, in Victoria West, at 8:00 A.M., and arriving at Nanaimo at 11:40. Southbound, the train left Nanaimo at 2:00 P.M. and arrived back at Russell's at 5:40.

By the end of its first fiscal year of operation, the following June 30, the Esquimalt and Nanaimo Railway had carried 13,000 passengers, producing $30,072.92, and 8,278 tons of freight, grossing $9,072.85. Mail and express brought the railroad another $2,744, and miscellaneous revenues raised the total gross earnings to $43,672.24. Company assets were $2,487,010.51, representing $1,200,000.00 in capital stocks, $750,000.00 in the Federal Government's subsidy, and $537,010.00 in other capital. The company owned four Schenectady built 4-4-0 locomotives, four passenger cars, three baggage and express cars, and 70 freight cars. In addition, Robert Dunsmuir had his own private car, *Maude.* The directors were pleased with the first year's operations.

In 1887, the E&N's tracks were extended from Nanaimo 4.8 miles north to Wellington, the site of the Dunsmuirs' vast mining operations. Wellington was the obvious northern terminus for the railroad, since it made it possible to provide a direct rail connection between the mines and the major domestic coal markets of Victoria and Esquimalt. The railroad could not ignore such a major source of revenue.

With regular service now a reality, Dunsmuir turned his attention to extending the railroad from Russell's to Victoria. The distance involved was less than one mile, but it was necessary to bridge part of Victoria's Inner Harbour to reach the outskirts of the business district. Work was completed and the bridge was officially opened on March 29, 1888. For three days prior to the event, the mechanical staff at Russell's was busy decorating and polishing locomotive No. 4, Dunsmuir's private

On March 29, 1888, the E&N's No. 4 pulled Robert Dunsmuir's private car *Maude*, three coaches and a combine into the downtown terminal of the Esquimalt and Nanaimo Railway in Victoria. As the *Daily Colonist* reported, it was, "a red letter day in Victoria's history—a day to be remembered by young and old alike for many years to come, an era in the progress and development of the city—the arrival of the first passenger train. The day was observed throughout the city generally as a half holiday, the public offices, schools, and business houses closing in honour of the event, and the public turning out en masse." Dunsmuir's car *Maude* had been Andrew Onderdonk's *Eva* during his construction of the Canadian Pacific Railway through the Fraser Canyon just a few years before.—PROVINCIAL ARCHIVES

So elated were the citizens of Victoria with the event that they built a decorated archway framing a picture of Robert Dunsmuir. A banner carried the words: "Long Looked For Come at Last." Another sign visible in the photograph said: "Welcome Dunsmuir" and "Victoria — New York." — PROVINCIAL ARCHIVES

car, *Maude,* and the three coaches that were to make up the official train. After train No. 1 had arrived from Nanaimo, the gaily decorated cars were backed onto the main line and coupled onto the cars from the regular train. Dignitaries, guests, and as many hangers-on as could be squeezed in boarded the train. With engineer Aaron Garland at the throttle, the No. 4 eased through Russell's and onto the new span, taking the train into Victoria. An excited crowd of 5,000, many of whom had awaited this moment for years, broke into loud cheering as the train reached the bridge. In the words of the *Daily Colonist* reporter, "This (the bridge crossing) was the signal for an outburst of enthusiasm never before heard in Victoria. Every whistle connected with the foundry, sawmill, rice mill, factories and steamers in the harbour commenced to toot, and amidst this pandemonium of sound, and with her own whistle blowing, and bells ringing, the first passenger train of the E&N crossed the swing bridge, snapping the ribbons stretching across her path like threads, and slowly steamed into the depot."

Dunsmuir triumphantly stepped down from the *Maude* and entered a waiting carriage. Then, "Just as the procession started from the depot the enthusiasm of the crowd broke forth afresh, and resulted in the horses being unhitched from the carriage ropes attached to the vehicle, and the employees of the Albion Iron Works (owned by Dunsmuir) taking hold insisted upon drawing the carriage by this means over the rest of the route." Dunsmuir was conveyed by his workers through the gaily decorated streets of Victoria to a banquet held in his honor.

Robert Dunsmuir's triumph was brief however. The following April he died after a short illness, and his sons, Alex and James were left to manage his vast interests. At the next meeting of the Esquimalt and Nanaimo Railway Company, Alex, still a resident of San Francisco, was elected president. James assumed full management of the Dunsmuirs' collieries.

Robert Dunsmuir's funeral was the largest ever witnessed on Vancouver Island. An estimated crowd of 10,000 to 14,000 people watched the solemn procession of 1,200 men move through the main streets of Victoria. Pallbearers included E&N conductors Black, Weldon, and Coburn, and Captains Christensen and Bendrot, and P. Hickey. Many of British Columbia's most distinguished citizens were honorary pallbearers. These included Joseph Hunter, E&N chief engineer and general manager, Victoria's Mayor Grant, and the Province's illustrious judge, Sir Matthew Begbie.

Under the capable management of Dunsmuir's sons, traffic increased steadily on the Esquimalt and Nanaimo Railway, and soon a motive power and equipment shortage was eminent. The need for new locomotives prompted the acquisition of a heavy Schenectady built 4-6-0. It was felt that the added power of this machine would be a great advantage on the grades over the Malahat between Victoria and Duncan. On May 3, 1890, the Southern Pacific Railroad delivered the 52-ton locomotive to the steamer *Wellington* at San Francisco. As the locomotive was being raised onto the deck of the steamer, the heavy tackle broke, and the E&N's newest engine was sent plunging through the ship's railing to the bottom of the harbour. It took three days to secure cables to the locomotive, submerged in 30 feet of water and covered with mud, and to raise it to the surface. The crews immediately set to work hosing down the machine before it could be corroded by the salt water. A song which was popular at that time included the line, ". . . McGinty went to the bottom of the sea." In good railroad tradition, the locomotive was promptly christened *McGinty,* unofficially of course. On July 8, E&N's No. 5, *McGinty,* made a trial run from Victoria to Malahat Station and back. The following week it was entered into regular service, and was to work on Vancouver Island for many years.

Wrecks due to errors in dispatching were not uncommon in the early days of railroading before radios and block signal systems were developed. The actions of one quick thinking conductor saved the E&N Railway a serious accident. On May 24, 1890, a five car excusion train received clearance from the dispatcher and pulled out of Victoria for Wellington. Every seat in the train was occupied by people returning home after the Victoria Day holiday. The dispatcher suddenly realized to his horror that a southbound excursion train was due to arrive in Victoria at any minute, and he had just cleared the northbound train onto the same single track main line! He had no way of contacting either train crew except by telephone at Cobble Hill, many miles north of where the two trains would meet.

As the northbound train gathered speed run-

E&N No. 7 pauses at Ladysmith with a miners' train northbound for Extension. In the early years of its operation, the E&N received considerable revenue from the coal trains serving the Wellington and Extension mines. Moreover, the daily miners' trains greatly increased the passenger traffic on the line. (RIGHT) Virtually every holiday called for special trains on the E&N. Frequently the public response to the excursions was so great that the ability of the railway to accommodate all of the passengers was taxed to the limit. — BOTH PROVINCIAL ARCHIVES

ESQUIMALT & NANAIMO RAILWAY

Dominion Day, July 1st, 1891.

TIME CARD FOR SPECIALS.

NORTH BOUND. READ DOWN.		SOUTH BOUND. READ UP.	
De. Victoria	5.30 P.M.	Ar. Victoria	8.58 P.M.
" Russell's	5.34 "	" Russell's	8.54 "
" Esquimalt	5.44 "	" Esquimalt	8.44 "
" Goldstream	6.09 "	" Goldstream	8.19 "
" Shawnigan L.	7.04 "	" Shawnigan L.	7.24 "
" COBBLE HILL	7.14 "	" COBBLE HILL	7.14 "
" McPherson's	7.29 "	" McPherson's	6.59 "
" Koksilah	7.39 "	" Koksilah	6.49 "
" Duncan's	7.44 "	" Duncan's	6.44 "
" Somenos	7.54 "	" Somenos	6.34 "
" Chemainus	8.16 "	" Chemainus	6.12 "
" Nanaimo	9.14 "	" Nanaimo	5.14 "
Ar. Wellington	9.29 "	De. Wellington	4.59 P.M.

Section Foremen will pass along the track ahead of these trains, clearing them at the end of their Sections by ten minutes only.

JOS. HUNTER,
GENERAL SUPT.

ning through Esquimalt, the conductor of the train remembered having read in the newspaper that a southbound train was scheduled to arrive in Victoria within the next few minutes. He immediately pulled the emergency cord and discussed the situation with the engineer. They agreed to run the train in reverse three miles back to the yards at Russell's and wait for the southbound train. They had been sidetracked only five minutes when the other train pulled into the yards. On seeing the southbound train reach Victoria, the frantic dispatcher nearly collapsed. When the northbound train later returned to Victoria, the conductor and engineer returned the train orders to the dispatcher so that there would be no record of the incident. Several years later however, the engineer of the train was to be dismissed due to a dispute with the railroad's master mechanic. At this time the conductor told James Dunsmuir of the incident, feeling that it should be considered before the engineer was fired. Dunsmuir agreed, and the engineer was not dismissed. The conductor would not name the dispatcher however, maintaining that he was not lodging a formal complaint against him.

On another occasion the train crews were less fortunate and a dispatching error led to a disastrous wreck. On September 18, 1900, at 10:30 A.M. the worst wreck in the history of the Esquimalt and Nanaimo Railway occurred two miles north of Ladysmith. Engine No. 10, a Baldwin 4-6-0, less than one year old, was working north towards Extension with empty mine cars on the E&N main line, having received clearance at Ladysmith. At the same time, the No. 1, the E&N's first locomotive, was running downgrade towards Ladysmith with a loaded coal train. "We were proceeding northward on the line, travelling about 35 miles an hour, when just rounding a bend, I saw the other train bearing down on us," related Fred Bland, engineer of the No. 10, for the *Victoria Daily Times* in December 1928. "I yelled to the engine crew to jump and they all got off all right. It seemed to me I would have a good chance if I stayed by the engine, but I decided against this just before the engines crashed, and I jumped from the deckplate of the locomotive. That was why I was injured. Somehow or other in the general mix up of flying debris which followed the crash nothing heavy landed on me, or I would not be telling you this story today. Four men who formed the engine crew of the other train were killed in the crash which badly wrecked the locomotives. We were lucky enough to escape."

The No. 1 was a total wreck, damaged beyond repair. The heavier No. 10 fared better. It was rebuilt and returned to service on the colliery trains. So great was the force of the impact that two of the loaded coal cars were thrown over the telegraph lines paralleling the tracks. The crew of the No. 1 had believed that the northbound train was on the siding at Ladysmith, waiting for them to clear, and they assumed the No. 1 to have open trackage for the rest of the run. Similarly, the crew of the No. 10 expected clear tracks after being dispatched from Ladysmith. Apparently, the operator at Ladysmith reported to train dispatcher, Fred Brown, that No. 1 had arrived. Brown then allowed the No. 10 to proceed. The operator at Ladysmith was held responsible for the wreck and served a term in jail for his negligence.

At the time of the accident, engines of the Esquimalt and Nanaimo Railway and the Wellington Colliery Railway carried identical numbers. It is

The head-on collision between E&N engines No. 1 and No. 10 was the worst wreck in the history of the railroad. In this photograph, taken shortly after the crash, the remains of the locomotives can be seen under the pile of wooden hopper cars. Steam is still escaping from the boiler of No. 1.—PROVINCIAL ARCHIVES (BELOW) The E&N's northbound and southbound dailies met at Duncan opposite the impressive Quamichan Hotel. Despite the annoyance of Victoria's clergy, E&N trains ran on Sundays. Dunsmuir is reported to have commented that he considered it a public benefit since it took those who did not attend church from the cities and removed them from evil influences.—PROVINCIAL ARCHIVES

believed that the operator at Ladysmith confused the Wellington Colliery's No. 1 with the Esquimalt and Nanaimo's No. 1 and told the dispatcher that the expected train had arrived, when in fact it was still several miles out on the main line. In any event, soon after the wreck, all the locomotives of the Wellington Colliery Railway were renumbered to insure that no further mistakes would occur.

Traffic volumes on the E&N rose throughout the 1890's, but revenues did not. In 1894, the railway carried 30,528 passengers and 51,992 tons of freight but ended the year with a deficit of $14,-491. In the fiscal year ending June 30, 1895, the situation was worse. There was a net loss of nearly $175,000. By 1898, the deficit had climbed to over $200,000. The year 1900, however, marked the turning point, when modest earnings of $5,440 were realized. After a few years of marginal gains, the E&N was able to maintain a profitable operation.

Passenger business following the turn of the century was brisk, averaging well over 100,000 fares annually. Passengers were accommodated in the company's seven modern open-vestibuled coaches and two beautifully appointed parlor cars, the *Ladysmith* and *Strathcona*. Equipped with lounge chairs and a private stateroom, the parlor cars provided the ultimate in comfort and luxury to travellers on Vancouver Island.

Innumerable excursion trains were run on the line. The most popular destinations for these specials were Goldstream and Shawnigan Lake, where

The Victoria terminal of the Esquimalt and Nanaimo presented a busy scene in the 1890's. In this view No. 4 is quietly steaming outside the freight shed. On the left is the Janion Hotel which housed the offices of the railway until 1944, and immediately behind the locomotive, the passenger depot. — PROVINCIAL ARCHIVES

One of the E&N's beautifully maintained 4-4-0's pauses with a northbound freight beside Shawnigan Lake. — PROVINCIAL ARCHIVES

A Vancouver Island photographer was fortunate to capture locomotive No. 5, the *McGinty*, on one of the numerous wooden trestles that characterized the E&N's line north of Victoria. On this special day in 1895 the locomotive is decorated in flags, evergreen and bunting, while the crew and passengers aboard the seven car train either step to a landing spot or poke their heads out of windows and look toward the photographer. — PROVINCIAL ARCHIVES

E&N No. 2 pulls a southbound train past the Nanaimo passenger station. Note that the locomotive features a number of turn of the century modifications including a straight stack, a new headlight and knuckle couplers. The last car in the train is the parlor car *Strathcona.* — NANAIMO MUSEUM

group picnics and other popular social events were held. Fares were low and the railroad was rewarded with heavy patronage. The E&N's excursions became eagerly anticipated events for residents all over southeastern Vancouver Island. Celebrations, local fairs, and holidays all called for special passenger trains. For example, the Cowichan Agricultural Exhibition at Duncan on September 28 and 29, 1900, required two extra trains. Fares for this holiday special from Victoria ranged from one to two dollars and bicycles were carried free of charge.

A suburban service was initiated to Shawnigan Lake during the summer months. It proved exceedingly popular for the residents in Victoria owning summer cottages at this beautiful lake. Daily trains would leave Victoria early in the evening and lay over at Shawnigan, making the return journey the next morning. This made it possible for workers to commute to Victoria while their families spent the summer at Shawnigan Lake. After the summer of 1907, this service was discontinued, to the sorrow of many of the residents.

During this time, the Esquimalt and Nanaimo Railway also operated a coastal service with the steamships, *City of Nanaimo* and *Joan.* Twice-weekly runs were made from Victoria to Union Bay near Cumberland via Nanaimo. Stopovers at smaller settlements on the Gulf Islands and Vancouver Island were arranged so that almost every coastal community had at least weekly service to Victoria and Nanaimo.

In 1900, Alex Dunsmuir died, leaving his entire estate to his brother, James. Two years later James was able to acquire the last outstanding shares in the Esquimalt and Nanaimo Railway, making himself sole owner of the prospering railway. On February 2, 1905, James Dunsmuir entered into negotiations with the Canadian Pacific Railway Company for sale of the Esquimalt and Nanaimo Railway. On June 8 of the same year the CPR

Because timber was cheap and readily available, nearly all of the bridges on the E&N were of wood construction. In later years most of these structures were replaced with steel spans or filled in. Here, a train eases across the Cowichan River just south of Duncan.—PROVINCIAL ARCHIVES

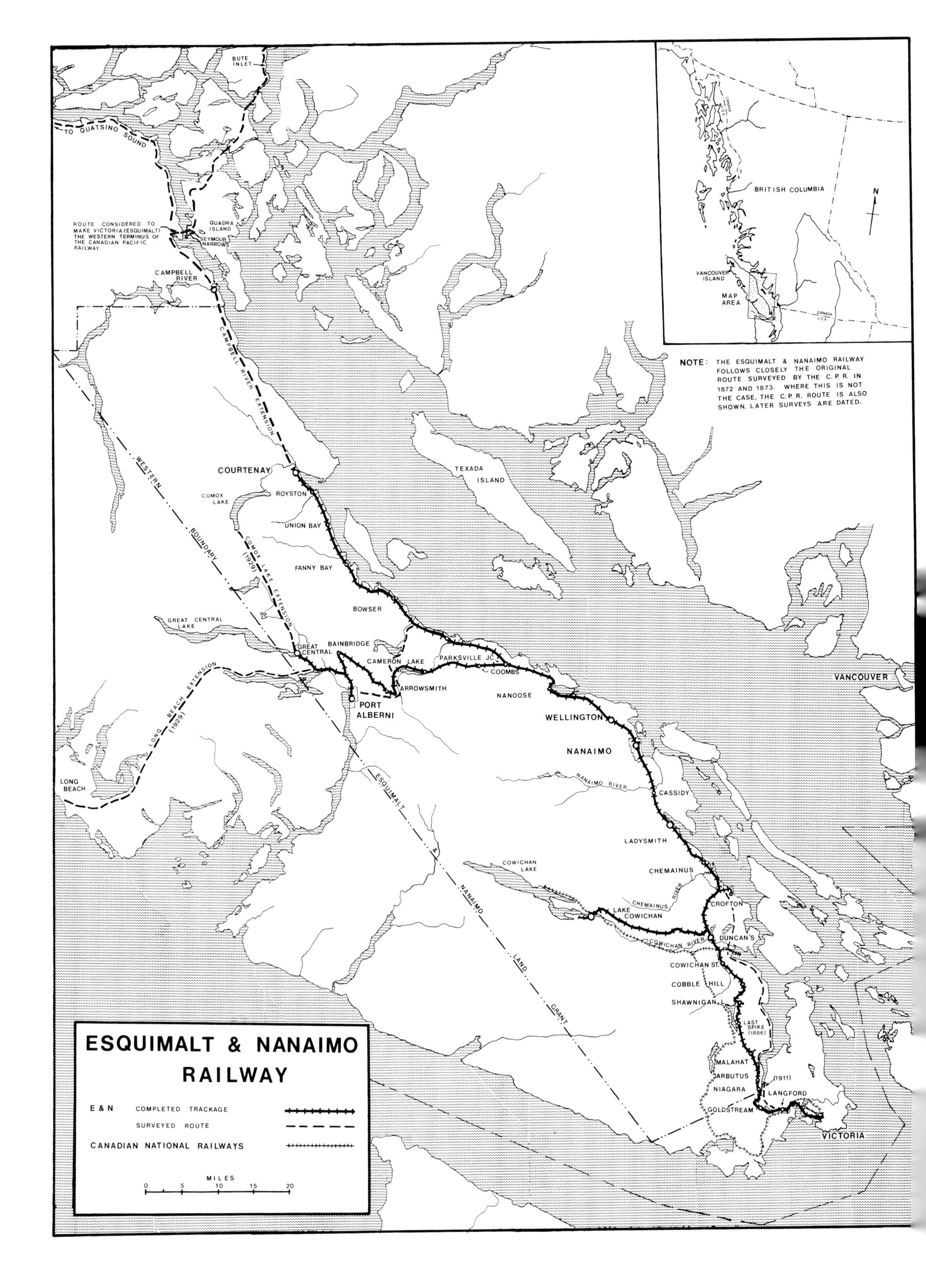
ESQUIMALT & NANAIMO RAILWAY
E & N COMPLETED TRACKAGE
SURVEYED ROUTE
CANADIAN NATIONAL RAILWAYS
MILES
0 5 10 15 20
NOTE: THE ESQUIMALT & NANAIMO RAILWAY FOLLOWS CLOSELY THE ORIGINAL ROUTE SURVEYED BY THE C.P.R. IN 1872 AND 1873. WHERE THIS IS NOT THE CASE, THE C.P.R. ROUTE IS ALSO SHOWN. LATER SURVEYS ARE DATED.
ROUTE CONSIDERED TO MAKE VICTORIA (ESQUIMALT) THE WESTERN TERMINUS OF THE CANADIAN PACIFIC RAILWAY.
BUTE INLET
TO QUATSINO SOUND
QUADRA ISLAND
SEYMOUR NARROWS
CAMPBELL RIVER
CAMPBELL RIVER EXTENSION
WESTERN BOUNDARY
COURTENAY
COMOX LAKE
ROYSTON
UNION BAY
COMOX LAKE EXTENSION (1929)
FANNY BAY
BOWSER
TEXADA ISLAND
GREAT CENTRAL LAKE
GREAT CENTRAL
BAINBRIDGE
CAMERON LAKE
PARKSVILLE JC.
COOMBS
ARROWSMITH
PORT ALBERNI
LONG BEACH EXTENSION (1929)
LONG BEACH
NANOOSE
WELLINGTON
NANAIMO
NANAIMO RIVER
CASSIDY
LADYSMITH
ESQUIMALT & NANAIMO LAND GRANT
COWICHAN LAKE
CHEMAINUS
CHEMAINUS RIVER
CROFTON
LAKE COWICHAN
DUNCAN'S
COWICHAN RIVER
COWICHAN ST.
COBBLE HILL
SHAWNIGAN L.
LAST SPIKE (1886)
MALAHAT
ARBUTUS
NIAGARA
(1911)
LANGFORD
GOLDSTREAM
VICTORIA
VANCOUVER
BRITISH COLUMBIA
N
VANCOUVER ISLAND
MAP AREA
CANADA
U.S.A.

purchased all of the E&N's assets, including the 78 mile railroad, steamships *City of Nanaimo* and *Joan,* a tugboat, the *Czar,* and the Esquimalt and Nanaimo Land Grant. In the transaction, Dunsmuir retained the coal and fire clay rights to the land grant property. The price finally agreed upon was $2,330,000, of which $1,080,000 was for the transportation system, while the balance covered the remaining 1,440,497 unsold acres of the land grant.

As a subsidiary company that was leased by Canadian Pacific Railways, the E&N retained its identity, if in name only. The leasing was not finalized until 1912, when a special act of the Provincial Legislature was passed ratifying an agreement reached between the CPR and the province to continue the tax-exempt status of the unsold parts of the Esquimalt and Nanaimo Railway's Land Grant. The CPR agreed to make a nominal annual payment to the province and to extend the railway north to the village of Courtenay by 1915. The land grant remained free of taxation until 1946 when British Columbia's Chief Justice Sloan ruled that this special exemption should cease.

With the railroad under CPR control, capital became available to begin a number of long desired improvements to the line. The numerous bridges presented many difficulties for the company. Their maintenance and repair contributed significantly to the early deficits incurred by the E&N. On December 16, 1890, flood water wrecked the Cowichan River bridge, severing the main line of the E&N just south of Duncan. High water in the river delayed reconstruction for many months, and it was not until November 6 of the following year that direct rail service between Victoria, Duncan, and points north was resumed. In the interim, trains met at the Cowichan River and passengers were transferred across by Indian dugout canoe. Freight was shipped from Victoria to Nanaimo by boat, then transferred to the E&N for movement to all points north of the break in the line.

Another major washout occurred on the E&N when the center section of the 260 foot high trestle over Niagara Canyon was carried away by a flash flood. As a result, the service was again interrupted between November 12, 1896, and January 28, 1897.

The beautiful station at Cameron Lake is no longer a feature of the E&N's line to Port Alberni, but when brand new CPR 4-6-0 No. 2460 stopped there in 1915 with the eastbound, it was a highlight not to be bypassed. — VANCOUVER PUBLIC LIBRARY

The first passenger train over the new and breathtaking line to Port Alberni was powered by 4-6-0 No. 494, shown here at the water stop of Apenes in a Leonard Frank photo. Mt. Arrowsmith is visible to the left above the beautiful stands of old growth Douglas-fir.— VANCOUVER PUBLIC LIBRARY

In May 1907 the CPR began work to upgrade the roadbed over the Malahat. The line was relaid with 60-pound rail, replacing the lighter 50 and 54-pound stock which had been in use since the opening of the railroad. In order to eliminate the costly maintenance of the many trestles along the route, a work crew was dispatched with a steam shovel to fill in as many of the bridges as possible. Even the spectacular bridge over Double Head Ravine at Mile 13 was filled in. Work was also undertaken to replace the wooden truss bridges over the Chemainus, Cowichan, and Nanaimo Rivers with concrete and steel spans. Subsequent programs saw the elimination of the spectacular wooden trestles at Niagara and Arbutus when steel structures were built across the canyons.

To further its upgrading program on the Esquimalt and Nanaimo, the CPR transferred two wooden observation cars to Vancouver Island for the daily passenger trains between Victoria and Wellington. The cars were actually the first two mountain observation cars placed in service by Canadian Pacific in the Rockies. Despite the fact that the cars were already 17 years old, local residents and tourists responded enthusiastically to them because they provided unobstructed views of the spectacular scenery along the railway. The cars were 57 feet long, had a seating capacity of 70, and weighed slightly less than 26 tons. On the E&N, they were named *Etobicoke* and *Bethlehem.* In later years, the two cars were acquired by the Western Fuel Company for use as miners' coaches on its Nanaimo coal mining railroad. One of them was eventually converted into an ambulance car for use in case of a mine disaster.

At the same time, the CPR began surveying and clearing to extend the line past Wellington. The planned route would carry the railway north to Parksville, where it would divide. One line would be laid north to Campbell River, on the northeast coast of Vancouver Island, and the other would extend west to Port Alberni on the west coast of the Island. The extension to Port Alberni was to be completed first, and then work was to proceed north of Parksville. By August 1908, the right-of-way to Parksville was cleared, and by the following year the eastern end of picturesque Cameron Lake, midway between Parksville and Port Alberni, had been reached. By 1910, track work had been completed to this point and passenger service was established. On December 20, 1911, the entire line to Port Alberni was opened and regular passenger service was inaugurated.

The new branch line passed through some of the most spectacular scenery on the whole of Vancouver Island. The 38.8 mile long Port Alberni subdivision climbs from sea level at the Alberni Inlet to an elevation of 1,284 feet at Locharkaig Summit 17 miles inland, where the descent to Parksville Junction begins. The maximum grade on line is 2.2 percent. The rugged terrain necessitated the use of numerous high trestles along the route. For several miles on the north shore of Cameron Lake, the tracks hug sheer cliffs several hundred feet above the water.

By August 6, 1914, 44.5 miles of the extension of the Victoria subdivision from Parksville to Campbell River had been completed. Daily passenger and express service was immediately extended to the end of track at the village of Courtenay. Grading and survey work continued on towards Campbell River, but World War I brought an end to construction, only eight miles past Courtenay.

The rapid expansion of the E&N prior to World War I required the addition of a number of new locomotives to the roster. Included were three 4-6-0's like No. 242 steaming through Stockett Junction on a passenger run. — ALBERT H. PAULL

Meanwhile in 1911, a branch line was constructed from Hayward Junction, north of Duncan, to the eastern end of Cowichan Lake to serve the growing logging industry in the area. This line, following the gradient of the Cowichan River, forms one of the steepest sections of the Esquimalt and Nanaimo Railway. Between Hayward Junction at Mile 0 and Sahtlam at Mile 9.2, the tracks climb nearly 570 feet on a steady two percent grade. The new branch line provided heavy traffic in logs and lumber between the lake and booming grounds and shipping facilities on the Straits of Georgia. In addition, local freight and passenger business supported a twice weekly mixed train between Lake Cowichan and Duncan.

The rapid extension of service on the Esquimalt and Nanaimo was quickly reflected in the growing locomotive roster of the company. Whereas in 1905, the company was operating only eight locomotives, by 1914, following the completion of the lines to Courtenay and Port Alberni, 23 were in service. Similarly, the number of passenger cars jumped from 11 to 43 during the same period.

As the photographs on these pages illustrate, the E&N made use of a number of types of Ten-Wheelers. In the above left action scene, the road's second No. 1 races by with a passenger train.—PROVINCIAL ARCHIVES (ABOVE) CPR Class C3a 4-6-0's operated on the E&N into the 1930's. No. 242 is shown outside the Victoria shops. — NORMAN GIDNEY (LEFT) Steaming quietly beside a large Marion shovel, No. 495 is in work train service at Bowser on the line to Courtenay. — H. J. BROWN

Moreover, as the CPR finalized the leasing of the Esquimalt and Nanaimo, many of the older E&N locomotives were replaced. In fact, only three locomotives of the Dunsmuir era were retained by the CPR. These were 4-6-0s Nos. 1, 5, and 6 which became CPR's 228, 227, and 229. All of the E&N's 4-4-0s were scrapped by 1913 as was the old No. 8, a Baldwin 0-6-0T built in 1878 as the *Premier* for the South Wellington Colliery Company's narrow gauge railway.

Locomotives transferred to the E&N from the CPR's mainland operations included representatives of a variety of classes of 4-6-0s. Among them were several compound locomotives. In these machines, the steam was used twice in an attempt to economize on fuel. The compound design was widely employed by many railroads around the turn of the century, but to the frustration of its advocates, any economy was offset by maintenance costs. As a result, most of these locomotives were rebuilt to conventional designs.

CPR locomotives transferred to the E&N included compounds, Nos. 497-499, which were rebuilt with single expansion cylinders in 1920-1923, and No. 458, later renumbered 358. The 358 was not rebuilt and was the last in service on the CPR system.

The E&N also received the CPR's 494-496 (Class D5) with simple cylinders, and compounds 240-242 (Class C3a) all of which were built at company shops in 1897 and D3h No. 7337 built in 1894. The 240-242 were soon rebuilt to single expansion engines. Crews found that the 240s had a tendency to slip when handling heavy trains, but generally considered them good locomotives. More popular were the heavier 490s which are remembered as responsive, powerful machines. Indeed, veteran E&N engineer Bob Brown found the 495 to be one of the best locomotives he ever handled. She was, "a real honey!" Both types of locomotive were normally assigned to freight service, but it was not uncommon for one or two to be found heading one of the railroad's passenger trains. The 494 even had the distinction of taking the first passenger train into Port Alberni when the branch was opened in 1911. The 490s stayed in regular service on the E&N until 1929 when they were all scrapped. Only the tender of No. 495 was saved, being converted into a water car for use during the summer forest fire season. The 240s were officially transferred to the Esquimalt and Nanaimo Railway in August 1913 and during the 1930's were lettered for the E&N, carrying road numbers 40-42. They were withdrawn from service in the late 1930's and were scrapped.

Most striking of the E&N's new locomotives were the six brand new D4g 4-6-0s numbered 2460-2465 (later renumbered 460-465). These machines handled the vast majority of all passenger movements on the railroad for nearly 30 years before they were retired or relegated to freight service during the early 1940's. They were particularly attractive locomotives. Their 62-inch drivers, Walschaert valve gear, and high-mounted boiler gave them a fast racy appearance. With 19 x 24-inch cylinders, they had adequate power to handle all but the longest excursion trains and were capable of considerable speed. One was unofficially clocked at over 60 miles per hour while wheeling a seven car passenger train along a straight stretch of line south of Courtenay.

Like the 240s, four of the D4g's were officially transferred to the E&N, although not until later years. They too carried E&N markings and road numbers during the 1930's, becoming E&N's Nos. 60-63. Nos. 464 and 465 were officially retained by CPR during this period and were not renumbered.

For yard service on the E&N, two 2-4-2 tank locomotives were ordered from Montreal Locomotive Works. The first, No. 1998, was outshopped in March 1910, and was followed in December 1911 by No. 1997, an identical engine with 14 x 22-inch cylinders and 44-inch drivers. Built as coal burn-

Shop crews on the Esquimalt and Nanaimo kept their locomotives spotless. Here, No. 62 and No. 63 pause at Parksville Junction with passenger trains bound for Courtenay and Port Alberni. The photograph shows the locomotives as they appeared during the 1930's when they were officially transferred from the CPR to the E&N and carried the name and numbers of the Vancouver Island line. — AUTHOR'S COLLECTION

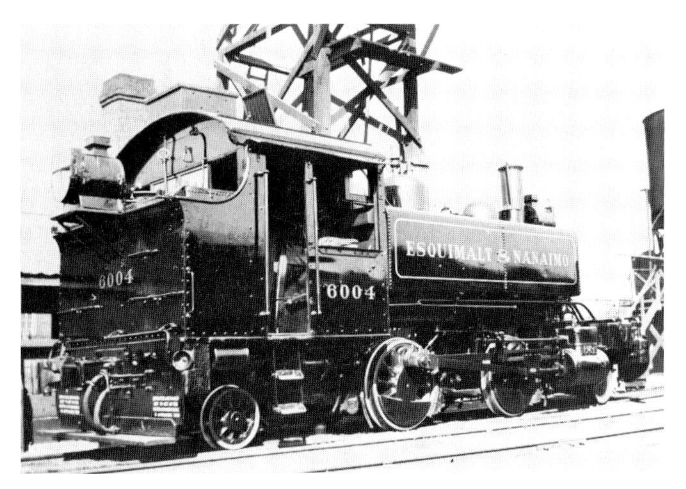

In 1910 and 1911, the Montreal Locomotive Works built the E&N's two unusual 2-4-2 type tank engines for yard service in Victoria. No. 6005 was identical to the No. 6004 as shown at the left. These locomotives were augmented and eventually superseded by heavy 0-6-0's during the 1930's.—ALBERT H. PAULL (BELOW) Canadian Pacific No. 6174 was one of the last steam switchers used on the E&N. Still well maintained, dieselization was only months away when this photograph was taken in 1948. — GERALD M. BEST COLLECTION

ers, they were later converted to burn oil as it became the practice of the E&N to operate only oil fired locomotives. In 1913, the two engines were renumbered 6004 and 6005. For a few years, the E&N also had the services of CPR's No. 1999, an old Rhode Island built 0-4-0T dating back to 1883 and No. 7163, an 1882 vintage 4-4-0 built by Dubs and Company of Glasgow, Scotland.

While this may seem like quite an impressive roster of locomotives for a small railroad like the Esquimalt and Nanaimo, there was little surplus power available. Two daily passenger trains between Victoria and Wellington, the daily connections to Port Alberni and Courtenay, a twice weekly service to Cowichan Lake and growing freight traffic on all sections of the railway kept most serviceable locomotives on the road.

January 1916 brought record snowfalls to Vancouver Island. Here, train crews are plowing out the E&N's main line through Duncan. — PROVINCIAL ARCHIVES

Until the automobile became the major means of travel, train time always brought large crowds to the station. In this scene, passengers gather around the E&N's daily train at Port Alberni. — Provincial Archives

Added traffic came to the E&N in 1925 when the Great Central subdivision, the last major extension of the railway, was opened. This line ran from Solly Junction north of Port Alberni to Great Central, 10.5 miles to the northwest. It was constructed to serve a large sawmill complex built by Great Central Sawmills Limited. Further extensions were planned to Long Beach on the west coast and to Comox Lake, but no construction work was ever undertaken on these lines.

In the early days of its operations, the Esquimalt and Nanaimo was isolated from the railroads on the mainland of British Columbia. When the interchange of cars was necessary, they were barged from Ladysmith or Esquimalt to various mainland points. In 1899, a car ferry slip was constructed at Ladysmith to serve both the Esquimalt and Nanaimo and the Wellington Colliery Railway, making possible the establishment of a regular interchange service with the Canadian Pacific Railway. The direct shipment of loaded cars resulted in considerable savings in time and money to the railroads. It eliminated the need for loading and unloading freight onto steamers for shipment to and from Vancouver Island. This reduction in handling also reduced the danger of damaging perishable or fragile merchandise.

An E&N passenger train, powered by No. 479 waits outside the depot at Port Alberni. In the background is Bloedel, Stewart and Welch's large sawmill where a five-masted schooner is loading lumber. — Provincial Archives

The ferry slip at Ladysmith remained the property of the Wellington Colliery Railway until 1920, when it was sold to the E&N. To facilitate the interchange of cars to and from points on the Alberni and Courtenay lines, another ferry slip was opened at Jayem (Nanoose Bay) north of Wellington on June 8, 1921. Following the CPR's acquisition of the Nanaimo waterfront property of Canadian Collieries (Dunsmuir) Limited in 1953, a new transfer slip and terminal were constructed there. Since that time, nearly all interchange traffic for Vancouver Island points on the E&N is directed through this facility. The E&N also interchanged cars with the Milwaukee Road through a ferry slip operated by Island Tug and Barge Limited in Victoria.

It should be mentioned that in addition to the Esquimalt and Nanaimo Railway the CPR has also operated an extensive coastal steamship service to and from Vancouver Island. The routes were between Vancouver and Nanaimo, where connections were made with E&N passenger trains, and between Victoria, Seattle, and Vancouver; the famous "triangle" service. The CPR's "Princess" ships, used on these operations, have always been maintained to a high standard and have often been referred to as miniature ocean liners. In addition, a number of smaller vessels were once employed in local service along the coasts of Vancouver Island. In the late 1950's, the CPR steamer service was greatly reduced. By the mid-1960's, only three of the passenger vessels remained on the Pacific coast. The *Princess of Vancouver* maintained a year-round service between Nanaimo and Vancouver, the *Princess Patricia* was used for summer cruises to Alaska and the *Princess Marguerite* operated each summer between Victoria, Port Angeles and Seattle. The *Marguerite* was acquired by the British Columbia Government in 1975 as was the *Vancouver* in 1981. The *Patricia* made its last Alaska cruise in 1981 and was eventually scrapped. The *Marguerite* and the *Vancouver* were later sold to the Stena Line which soon retired the *Marguerite* and ended its service between Victoria and Seattle in 1990.

Retired from the CPR's British Columbia Coast Steamship Service in the early 1960's, the *Princess Elaine* and *Princess Louise* were laid up in Victoria before being sold for restaurant vessels. (RIGHT) The *Princess Marguerite* was the last steamship running on the Pacific coast when finally retired in 1989. The beautiful vessel was still in summer service between Victoria and the Washington State ports of Seattle and Port Angeles when photographed waiting to take on passengers in Victoria. The *Marguerite* was scrapped in 1996.—BOTH HARRE DEMORO

The parlor car *Malahat* brings up the rear of a four-car E&N passenger train headed by D4g Ten-Wheeler No. 462. The train is starting across the high steel bridge over Arbutus Canyon. — Ted Robson Collection

Passenger service provided a major source of revenue on the Esquimalt and Nanaimo before the depression years. With total net earnings for the railroad averaging between a quarter and a half million dollars a year from the end of World War I to the early 1920's, the CPR began a program to modernize the passenger equipment used on the E&N. In 1923 electrically lit equipment was tested and made operational, and the following year a parlor car named *Malahat* was placed in service. New for the E&N, *Malahat* had already run many miles for the CPR. The car was built at the CPR's Hochelaga Shops in April 1893, as the sleeping car *Calcutta,* being renamed *Palgrave* in 1918. Five years later, in December 1923, it was rebuilt and converted to a parlor car, sold to the E&N and renamed *Malahat.* Its career was far from over, for it served on the E&N until 1952 when it was returned to the CPR and converted into an instruction car (No. 56). Finally, in 1960, the car was donated to the Canadian Railroad Historical Association. *Malahat* was followed in 1927 by the newer *Qualicum.* This car was built at CP's Angus Shops in November 1913 as the parlor car *Assiniboine,* whose name was changed to *Annonciation* in 1918 and then simply No. 6722 late the following year. *Qualicum's* later history is unclear, but it probably ended its days as Instruction Car 55

A racy E&N 4-6-0 wheels the southbound No. 2 away from the Courtenay station and picks up speed for the run to Parksville Junction. — Ted Robson

Casting long shadows, the 463 pulls through the Victoria yards with the Nanaimo passenger train in 1927. The train consisted of a mail and express car, a baggage car, two coaches and a stateroom-equipped parlor car.—CYRIL LITTLEBURY—AUTHOR'S COLLECTION

after being withdrawn from service on the E&N. Open vestibule coaches, baggage and express cars continued in service on the E&N into the 1930's, when somewhat more up-to-date wooden cars were assigned to the railway's passenger trains.

However, the E&N was not without competition for its lucrative passenger business. Indeed, by the late 1920's, Vancouver Island Coach Lines was operating a bus service which attracted increasing numbers of travellers away from the railway. The buses ran three round trips a day between Victoria and Nanaimo. The one way trip took three hours and 45 minutes, comparing favorably with the schedule maintained by the E&N's passenger trains. A service was also operated to Port Alberni and Courtenay from Nanaimo. Two return trips a day were run to each city. While the buses certainly could not compete with the trains for comfort, their schedule was actually more frequent. As newer and more modern buses were acquired, and as the roads were improved, the E&N began to see a noticeable loss in its business. Private cars were also becoming more and more common throughout the years between the two world wars, and caused a further decline in railroad travel. Wartime restrictions on the construction of private automobiles and rationing of gas gave the railroad passenger service a brief and

Still in immaculate condition after over 30 years of service on the CPR, Ten-Wheeler No. 442 pauses at Parksville Junction on a bright spring day in 1947.—GERALD M. BEST COLLECTION

welcome surge, but the general decline continued after World War II.

Meanwhile, 2-8-0s had taken over much of the freight traffic from the E&N's aging fleet of 4-6-0s. The Consolidations handled main line tonnage over the Malahat and Alberni summits, worked log trains from Cowichan, moved coal from the mines at Nanaimo, South Wellington, and Cumberland, and powered local freights all over the system. The CPR operated two types of 2-8-0 on its Esquimalt and Nanaimo subsidiary. They were built in the late 1890's by the CPR at its own shops or by the Baldwin, Richmond or Canadian Locomotive Companies. The older machines, numbered in the 3100s, of Class L3 and L5, were nearing the end of their careers when assigned to the E&N. They were deckless, making conditions in the engine cab very crowded and uncomfortable. They carried slide valves, and some even sported wooden pilots. Three of these locomotives, Nos. 3130-3132, were officially transferred to the E&N and carried Nos. 30-32 during the early 1930's. By 1935, most of the 3100s had been replaced by a second type of 2-8-0, which was more modern and slightly heavier, although built in the same period. Locomotives of this type were numbered in the 3200 series and were CPR Class M1

Locomotive No. 3182, which is representative of the E&N's older classes of 2-8-0s, was built by the Canadian Pacific in 1899. These locomotives served on the E&N into the 1930's before they were retired and scrapped. (BELOW) An old workhorse on the E&N, the No. 3131, snorts into Nanaimo with a freight from Victoria. Heavy traffic would occasionally call for two of the L3 and L5 Consolidations to doublehead freights over the Malahat.—BOTH ALBERT H. PAULL

At Wellington, in a scene typical of the mid-1930's, two of the E&N's 3200 series Consolidations wait for the next freight assignment. — Albert H. Paull

Stockett Junction near Nanaimo was the interchange point between the E&N and the colliery operations at Nanaimo. In the scene above, from 1930, CPR No. 3241 pulls into the yard as Canadian Collieries (Dunsmuir) Ltd.'s No. 8 waits to pick up the hopper cars to be switched down to the docks. — Albert H. Paull (BELOW) Well maintained No. 3229 is serviced at Victoria in 1940. — Norman Gidney

and M2 machines. Over the years, nearly two dozen of these engines were assigned to the E&N for varying periods of time.

The 3200s were the mainstay of the freight locomotive pool until 1940 when the CPR began to replace nearly all road engines on the E&N with D10 class 4-6-0s. Between 1905 and 1912, Canadian Pacific Railway ordered over 500 D10s and used them in nearly every part of Canada from Nova Scotia in the East to Vancouver Island in the West. They were sturdy, powerful locomotives and performed a dual service role on the E&N taking over nearly all freight and passenger runs. They operated with equal facility on slow log

On the high steel bridge over Arbutus Canyon an E&N D10 Ten-Wheeler works a long freight towards Malahat Station and the summit of the grade north of Victoria. — JOHN NEWMAN

Looking as if it were suspended in the trees, No. 914 steams across the Niagara Canyon bridge. — John Newman

CPR D10 4-6-0's were the last class of steam locomotives to be assigned to the E&N. During the 1940's they took over nearly all of the freight and passenger runs on the line. In this action scene at Arbutus Canyon No. 923 leads the daily passenger train towards Nanaimo. — John Newman

Looking at CPR No. 925, pictured at Victoria, it is difficult to believe that the locomotive was 38 years old when photographed in 1948. — Gerald M. Best Collection

E&N public timetables were produced in a variety of designs over the years. Particularly interesting here is the E&N elk emblem and the prominent display of the open-platform parlor car. — AUTHOR'S AND GOLDEN WEST COLLECTION

trains or on one of the line's ever popular excursions.

January 1935 brought heavy snowfalls to Vancouver Island. In places, drifts up to 15 feet deep covered the tracks, presenting enormous obstacles to a railroad accustomed to only a few inches of snow each winter. Frequent fast trains managed to keep most of the line open. North of Duncan train service was maintained throughout the entire period of the storm. To the south, however, a major washout and slide occurred which required round-the-clock work by repair crews.

On January 24, a disaster was averted by the alert response of engineer Harry Austin. While nearing Nanoose Bay, where the tracks were obscured by several feet of fresh snow, Austin noticed a stream of gravel coming through a snow guard. Immediately he set the emergency brakes, and brought his fast moving passenger train to a halt. Upon further investigation, he found a 45-foot long section of unsupported track covered by snow hanging over a 15-foot deep washout barely 50 feet in front of the locomotive. North and southbound trains met at the washout and exchanged passengers and express within an hour, and it was possible for passengers to make connections to the mainland via CPR steamship from Nanaimo. Soon after, another washout occurred near Wellington. Crews were rushed to the scene and within six hours a temporary bridge was built making it possible for 750 tons of badly needed coal to be shipped to Vancouver with only a slight delay.

World War II brought increased traffic in both freight and passengers to the Esquimalt and Nanaimo. It also presented problems in finding sufficient men to maintain and operate the line. By fall, 1942, increasing labour shortages prompted the E&N to begin employing women to work at the company's shops. The ladies received a wage of $100 a month and were assigned to engine wiping, washing down boilers, car inspection and cleaning, and laying-up rolling stock. The *Colonist* reported that they were being trained by competent instructors and that they were learning quickly, "quite a contrast to the type of male youth generally employed for this particular work."

After the war, freight traffic remained high on the E&N, with an average of 33,500 car loads originating on Vancouver Island each year. Of these, 14,500 were destined for points on the mainland. Balanced against only 7,600 incoming loads, this reflected the E&N's dependence on export traffic in coal and forest products for a substantial part of its revenues. In fact, when log hauling and other local operations are considered, 95 percent of all freight carried on the railroad during the late 1940's came from the mining and forest industries.

The post-war years saw the CPR begin an extensive program of modernizing its rolling stock

In January 1949, the newest thing on the E&N was CPR No. 8002. It was the first of 13 Baldwin diesel road-switchers to be assigned to the E&N that year. These locomotives quickly took over all operations on the E&N and made the CPR's Vancouver Island operations the first in Canada to be fully dieselized. — JOHN NEWMAN

In the mid-1950's, the E&N built new yards and diesel facilities on the site of the old Nanaimo colliery operations. The terminal was named Wellcox and serves trains running to Courtney, Port Alberni, and Cowichan Lake. — ROBERT D. TURNER

and locomotive fleet. In 1948, as a part of this program, the company placed an order with the Canadian Locomotive Company for 13 Baldwin built 1,000 h.p. diesel road-switchers. It was the intention of the CPR to use these locomotives to completely dieselize the E&N rather than merely supplementing the existing steam locomotives with a few diesel units. It was felt that Vancouver Island would provide an ideal testing ground for main line dieselization. With the arrival of the new Baldwins early in 1949, the E&N became the first division of the CPR to be completely dieselized.

The first unit to reach the E&N after servicing in Vancouver was No. 8002, followed soon after by the remaining 12, numbered between 8000 and 8012. Several trial runs were made, and on January 24, 1949, engineer Walter A. Flude operated the first regularly scheduled diesel powered freight on Vancouver Island, pulling 23 cars from Victoria to Wellington. Within a few months, the steam locomotive had become a thing of the past on the Esquimalt and Nanaimo Railway. Since there were still large numbers of CPR steam locomotives active on the mainland of British Columbia, most of the E&N's steam engines were transferred there for continued operation. The older machines, such as the surviving 3200s, were sold for scrap. The fact that 13 diesels could fulfill the functions performed by 20 steam locomotives is a clear indication of the economies the railroads realized by turning to the diesel.

Other changes to the E&N's operations came during the 1950's. Wellington, long abandoned as a coal mining center, had remained an important terminal for the railway throughout the early postwar years. It served as a terminus for the daily freight crews operating to and from Victoria and for crews operating to Courtenay and Port Alberni. In addition, it served the crew of the coal train running to South Wellington and Storms. With the closure of the Nanaimo mines in 1953, the CPR took over the rail connection from Stockett Junction to the Nanaimo waterfront and built a new terminus and car ferry dock on the site of the old colliery operation. Wellcox, as the new facility was called, was placed in operation in June 1955 and became the main terminal of the railway north of Victoria. The facilities at Wellington were abandoned and the nearby ferry slip at Jayem on Nanoose Bay was relegated to standby

Blasting upgrade, two Baldwin road-switchers lead E&N train No. 51 northbound toward the summit of the Malahat. The roar of the exhaust from the laboring diesels is nearly deafening but momentarily there will be quiet as the train plunges into the only tunnel on the Esquimalt and Nanaimo. — Robert D. Turner

Diesel-hydraulic switcher No. 15 was a familar sight in the E&N's Victoria yards during the 1960's. Lacking the power for the heavier switching jobs, the unit was eventually relegated to standby service and then sold. — RICHARD R. HORNE

Baldwin No. 8004 pilots a fast-moving extra over the Nanaimo River.—ROBERT D. TURNER (LEFT) On the line to Courtenay near Mud Bay, E&N train No. 65 is encountering drifts of new wet snow in this scene from a December 1970 storm. — JOHN HOFFMEISTER

The E&N is not usually plagued by much snow in the winter, but every few years, as in January 1969, a cold spell hits and drifts pile up on the Malahat and on the Port Alberni line. After bucking heavy snows over the Malahat, the snow plow train has just arrived in Victoria where the crew will take a short break for supper while the train is turned and readied for the return trip to Nanaimo.—ROBERT D. TURNER

Eighty-four years after Robert Dunsmuir rode the first passenger train across the Johnson Street Bridge into Victoria, E&N passenger trains discontinued operations into the old terminal. Subsequently the *Dayliner* ran from a new station built near the site of the original Russell's depot. The Victoria Station, shown in the background of this picture, was torn down late in 1972. In 1985 a new station was built at this location and *Dayliner* service once again reached downtown Victoria.—ROBERT D. TURNER

service. The closure of the E&N's Wellington terminal marked the end of a long era of close association between the railway and the town built by Robert Dunsmuir. After 1955, Wellington was only a flag stop for the daily passenger trains.

By the mid-1950's, passenger service on the E&N had been cut back to only one return trip a day between Victoria and Courtenay and a daily connection to Port Alberni from Parksville. The Port Alberni service was downgraded to a mixed train, and a long layover was required for passengers wishing to make the connection from Victoria.

In September 1955, a Budd built rail diesel car (RDC) was placed in service on Vancouver Island, replacing the E&N's obsolete standard passenger equipment. RDC service began September 12, with one coach making a return trip to Courtenay from Victoria each weekday. The reduction in travel time was significant. Whereas in 1949 it took 6 hours and 50 minutes to travel the 140 miles between Victoria and Courtenay, in 1955 the RDC reduced the time to 4 hours and 10 minutes. Soon after the inauguration of this service, the Alberni mixed train was dropped from the schedule.

During the 1960's, all of the road-switchers were equipped for multiple unit operations, making possible the running of heavier trains and reductions in the number of train crews employed on the E&N. In peak traffic periods, Baldwin yard diesels of the CPR's 7065 to 7075 series, equipped

Fog has closed in over the mountains as a northbound E&N *Dayliner* passes the long unused water tower at Malahat Station. It is the day after Christmas, 1969. — ROBERT D. TURNER

North of Ladysmith the E&N crosses the line of the Comox Logging and Railway Company. (LEFT) The Armstrong plant housed in the two story building is used to control signals at this interchange. — BOTH ROBERT D. TURNER

Koksilah, south of Duncan, is a typical flag stop on the E&N. — ROBERT D. TURNER

Dieselization of passenger services on the E&N did not bring an end to the operation of excursions so popular since the opening of the railway in the 1880's. In the scene above, *Dayliner* No. 9023 crosses one of the numerous trestles on the spectacular Port Alberni line. The special train was operated for the Juan de Fuca Railroad Club in 1969. (LEFT) The schedule for the E&N's *Dayliner* is posted on the wall of the Victoria depot. — BOTH ROBERT D. TURNER

Across Cameron Lake, an E&N freight climbs towards the summit of the line to Port Alberni. The train is powered by two General Motors GP-9 road-switchers. This type of diesel locomotive has replaced the older Balwins on the Port Alberni subdivision during the summer months since it was found that the dynamic brakes of the GM units reduced the danger of fires along the right-of-way. — ROBERT D. TURNER

Freshly repainted in the vibrant new CP Rail colors, No. 8001 leads two other Baldwins through Langford with train No. 51, the daily northbound freight from Victoria. — ROBERT D. TURNER

At Wellcox, the E&N's Herb Murray keeps track of train movements and prepares train orders and clearances for freights operating out of the Nanaimo terminal.—ROBERT D. TURNER

for road service, have been used on Vancouver Island. Initially, two were used on the Cowichan branch to handle log trains, but since then, the 7000s have made frequent appearances on all parts of the E&N. For several years, the 7074 was employed in switching the yards at Victoria. Recently, however, a Montreal Locomotive Works yard diesel has taken over these duties.

December 1969, marked the advent of *CP Rail,* the name chosen to succeed Canadian Pacific Railway, on Vancouver Island. At this time, the 8003 appeared in the bright red-orange color scheme symbolic of the company's new image for the 1970's. While the diesels may have had a face-lifting, the basic operations of the railroad remain little changed since the late 1940's when diesels first appeared on Vancouver Island.

Beginning in the early 1960's, the CPR sought permission to abandon passenger service on Vancouver Island. In the face of improved highways and the increased use of automobiles, the Dayliner was showing consistent losses. However, there was general opposition to any move to curtail services, and it was maintained that poor service was the principal cause of deficits in the passenger train operations. The findings of a Canadian Transport Commission investigation in 1970 reinforced these claims. The Commission found the passenger stations to be badly in need of repair. Indeed, one of its inspectors put his foot through a station platform. Additionally, it was found that the type of Dayliner being used provided inadequate passenger accommodation. Overflow crowds at peak periods were often seated in the baggage compartment. The scheduling was also found to be unsatisfactory for making ferry connections to the mainland. The Commission found that "the effort that is being made to render the service profitable is almost non-existent." The Commission ordered that these failings be rectified and that the service continue.

CP Rail improved scheduling, structures and advertising, assigning an RDC with larger passenger capacity, and in the summer placed a second Dayliner in service. Controversy, legal actions and deficits remained part of the Dayliner story, but these improvements and the enthusiasm of the Dayliner crews and its supporters carried the passenger service through to the creation of VIA and the next decades of operation described in Chapter VI.

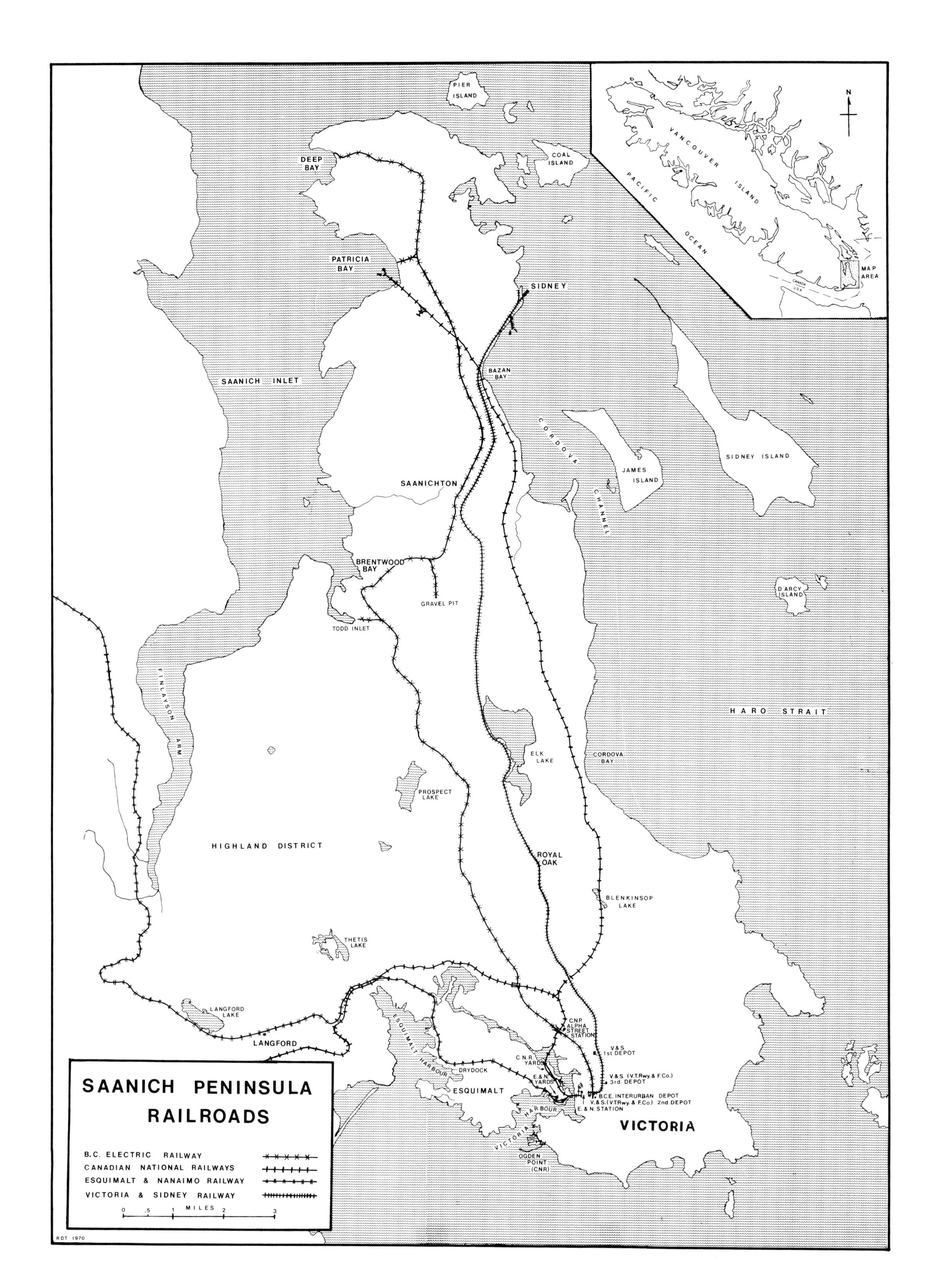

SAANICH PENINSULA
RAILROADS
B.C. ELECTRIC RAILWAY
CANADIAN NATIONAL RAILWAYS
ESQUIMALT & NANAIMO RAILWAY
VICTORIA & SIDNEY RAILWAY
0 .5 1 MILES 2 3
RDT 1970
PIER ISLAND
COAL ISLAND
DEEP BAY
PATRICIA BAY
SIDNEY
SAANICH INLET
BAZAN BAY
CORDOVA CHANNEL
JAMES ISLAND
SIDNEY ISLAND
SAANICHTON
BRENTWOOD BAY
GRAVEL PIT
TODD INLET
D'ARCY ISLAND
FINLAYSON ARM
HARO STRAIT
ELK LAKE
CORDOVA BAY
PROSPECT LAKE
HIGHLAND DISTRICT
ROYAL OAK
BLENKINSOP LAKE
THETIS LAKE
LANGFORD LAKE
LANGFORD
CNR ALPHA STREET STATION
V&S 1st. DEPOT
C.N.R. YARDS
E.& N. YARDS
DRYDOCK
ESQUIMALT HARBOUR
ESQUIMALT
V&S (V.T.Rwy.& F.Co.) 3rd. DEPOT
B.C.E. INTERURBAN DEPOT
V.&S.(V.T.Rwy.& F.Co.) 2nd. DEPOT
E.& N. STATION
VICTORIA HARBOUR
VICTORIA
OGDEN POINT (CNR)
N
VANCOUVER ISLAND
PACIFIC OCEAN
MAP AREA
CANADA
USA

3

SAANICH PENINSULA RAILROADS

THE SAANICH Peninsula is a narrow projection of land extending 20 miles north from Victoria at the southern end of Vancouver Island. The land, largely submerged under the ocean in the period following glaciation, is generally flat and rolling and is considered to be well suited for agricultural purposes. In many cases, low lying areas are occupied by shallow lakes and marshes. A number of low hills ranging from a few hundred to a thousand feet in elevation rise above the rolling landscape.

At the time of the first settlements on Vancouver Island, the Saanich Peninsula was mainly forested, but its potential as agricultural land was soon realized. As Fort Victoria developed into a major city, a number of small communities, including Royal Oak, Keatings, Brentwood Bay, Saanichton, and Sidney, were established on the peninsula.

Towards the end of the 1800's, people became increasingly railroad conscious. The iron horse had been a critical consideration in the union of British Columbia with the rest of Canada, and was the most important single factor in the settling of large parts of Western Canada. Residents of the Saanich Peninsula saw great possibilities of expanding settlement and industry if a railroad could be built from Victoria north through the growing Saanich communities. It was in this setting that the three railroads built on the Saanich Peninsula had their beginnings. Two — the Victoria and Sidney Railway and the British Columbia Electric Railway — are discussed in this chapter, while the third, built by the Canadian Northern Pacific Railway and later operated by Canadian National Railways, is detailed in the following chapter.

Several early proposals for railroads to serve the Saanich Peninsula were developed, but it was not until 1892 that a scheme acceptable to the City Council of Victoria was put forward. In that year, the Victoria and Sidney Railway Company proposed to build a standard gauge railroad from Victoria through the center of the Saanich Peninsula to the village of Sidney. The company asked the city for certain tax concessions and that three percent of the five percent interest payments on the company's $300,000 mortgage be guaranteed. The Provincial Government was requested to guarantee the remaining two percent annual payment.

The new company soon began surveying and grading the right-of-way. Though something less than ideal from an operational point of view, it passed through nearly every important community north of Victoria on the peninsula. In 1894, when the railroad was opened, Saanich was still largely

In the pastoral scene on the left, V&S 4-4-0 No. 2 with a short mixed train steams through the quiet farm lands of the Royal Oak area north of Victoria. The No. 2 was the oldest locomotive on the V&S roster, having been built in 1875. — PROVINCIAL ARCHIVES

forested, with only limited areas under cultivation. Timber and cordwood production was a key industry in the area, and provided a major source of freight revenue for the railroad. Since all of the early V&S locomotives were wood-burners, local residents quickly dubbed the train the "Cordwood Limited." A slightly less complimentary name for it was the "tri-weekly," because although it ran every day, it tried weakly.

In the early days of its operations, the V&S proved a popular route for excursion passengers to the agricultural fairs at Saanichton and for picnickers travelling to Bazan Bay and other scenic areas of the Saanich Peninsula. This was before the days of serious competition from buses and automobiles, and, since the roads existing at that time were in very poor condition, the train was by far the most popular means of travel.

It had always been hoped by promoters of the V&S that it could be connected to the mainland by steamer, with new rail lines built to the major Fraser Valley centers. This seemed to be a logical course for the V&S to follow, since it would then be made a major inter-city route instead of just a local line serving the Victoria area. In 1900, the idea was officially advanced, and by the following year, the Victoria Terminal Railway and Ferry Company had been formed. Under the charter of the new company, tracks were extended from the V&S terminus at Topaz Avenue to Cormorant Street in downtown Victoria, near city hall. Further plans were formulated to extend the tracks to the Esquimalt and Nanaimo Railway depot at Victoria, in order to provide a continuous rail connection with other Vancouver Island points. However, agreement could not be reached with the E&N and no work was undertaken on this project.

With the *Cordwood Limited* in tow, V&S No. 1 is about to leave the dock at Sidney. The appearance of this locomotive was changed in later years by the installation of a new headlight and knuckle couplers. — PROVINCIAL ARCHIVES

The speedy steamer *Victorian* shown above sailing from Victoria, was purchased for the V&S and converted into a car ferry to run from Sidney to Port Guichon. Overpowered and generally uneconomical to operate since its construction in 1891 for the Oregon Railway and Navigation Company, it maintained its reputation as a money loser on the V&S connection. It was withdrawn from service in 1905 after only two years of operation.—PROVINCIAL ARCHIVES

Victoria Terminal Railway and Ferry Company

S. S. "VICTORIAN"

BREAKFAST

CEREALS

Rolled Oats

FISH

Broiled Mackerel

BREAKFAST DISHES

Grilled Spring Chicken

HOT BREADS

SATURDAY, JULY 23RD 1904

Despite the problems she created for her owners, the *Victorian* was a comfortable ship and her menus could tempt even the most discriminating palate. — E. W. BARLOW COLLECTION

While work was progressing on the mainland section of line, known as the Liverpool and Canoe Pass Railway, which would connect with ferries running to Sidney, both the Victoria and Sidney Railway Company and the Victoria Terminal Railway and Ferry Company were purchased by the Great Northern Railway Company. Under Great Northern ownership, a modified mainland rail connection was completed. The Liverpool and Canoe Pass Railway right-of-way was abandoned in favor of a more southerly route from Port Guichon (near the present site of Ladner) to Cloverdale, on the New Westminster Southern Railway, another Great Northern subsidiary. A steamer, the S.S. *Victorian,* was purchased and converted into a car ferry for the Sidney to Port Guichon run. It was placed in service early in 1903.

At this time, the Canadian Pacific Railway had in operation the luxurious steamer, *Princess Victoria,* making daily runs between Victoria and Vancouver. The service was fast, reliable, and convenient, and as a result, few passengers used the Victoria Terminal Railway and Ferry Company's connections to the mainland. In early 1905, the *Victorian* was withdrawn from service.

Early maps of the Ladner area show plans for an extension of the Port Guichon to Cloverdale line south from Port Guichon to Tsawwassen Beach. There, a causeway or trestle was to be con-

Competition for the Victoria Terminal Railway and Ferry Company came from the peerless CPR steamer *Princess Victoria,* the fastest, most luxurious vessel on the coast. — PROVINCIAL ARCHIVES

structed to carry the trains out over the tidal flats to deep water, where a ferry could dock. Had this line been built, it would have substantially reduced the length of the ferry run to Vancouver Island. It is interesting to note that half a century later, a fast automobile ferry service was established between Tsawwassen Beach and Swartz Bay, north of Sidney, by the British Columbia Provincial Government.

The sternwheeler *Strathcona* and other steamers of the Sidney and Nanaimo Navigation Company connected with V&S trains at Sidney to provide a convenient service to and from the Gulf Islands. This photograph shows the Sidney wharf of the Victoria & Sidney. — Provincial Archives

Local traffic on the Victoria and Sidney Railway remained moderately heavy over the next few years, but the railroad was suffering from a pressing shortage of motive power and equipment, and money was not available to purchase the necessary additions. The service generally deteriorated; engine breakdowns and delays were prevalent. The local press became indignant, as can be seen from the following quote from the *Victoria Daily Colonist*, June 1, 1907.

The antiquated little locomotive that is without companion of any kind to share the burden of traffic on the Victoria and Sidney Railway grows weaker as it grows older, and its many sympathizers are becoming concerned as to its ability to stand the strain much longer . . . The promise of improvements . . . seems to be further away from realization than ever. The wharf at Sidney trembles and sways under the weight and motion of the train, while the teredos continue their deadly work on the sickly pilings. Yesterday afternoon, the aged locomotive was called upon to make a desperate struggle to get itself and four cars off the wharf. The last car was still on the wharf when the engine became stalled on the grade leading to the main line. The train was allowed to run back onto the

Old and cantankerous, No. 2 was not much of an asset on the railroad. The locomotive was rather antiquated when acquired by the railway and saw little service after the arrival of locomotive No. 3. — Provincial Archives

wharf and after a suitable lapse of time, while steam pressure was raised, a second attempt was successfuly made with the little engine snorting with all the fury of a mogul at the head of a transcontinental freight as inch by inch it crawled up the track onto the main line.

The motive power situation on the V&S was not quite as bad as the above quote would indicate. The No. 1, a 2-6-0, which had been acquired new from the Canadian Locomotive Company in 1893, was well suited to the local service and was the mainstay of the railroad. The No. 2 was a much older 4-4-0, having been built in 1875. The machine's large drivers made it slippery on the grades, so that it could be assigned only to the lightest trains. The company's No. 3 was another 4-4-0, but better suited to the rolling grades of the V&S. It had originally been the Victoria Lumber and Manufacturing Company's No. 1, before being bought by the Vancouver Westminster and Yukon Railway, which eventually transferred her to the V&S. It would appear that the *Colonist* reporter formulated his observations on the railroad when two of the company's three locomotives were out of service.

The promise that the Great Northern Railway Company saw in the V&S when it purchased the line never really materialized. Profits during the early years were marginal, never adequate to justify any significant new investments in the property. As the service deteriorated, patrons grew more and more indignant, and the management of the line was scathingly criticized by the press.

Our understanding of the case is that the Great Northern Railway company is the virtual owner of the line. It is said that salaries are paid by Great Northern checks. We assume that in some way or other the Great Northern Railway is responsible for the abominable service with which the people of Saanich have to put up, and we say as emphatically as we know how that if any person or body corporate or any one else has any authority to bring the owners of the line to time, it is their duty to take the necessary steps without delay.

The charges against the railway are first that their cars are not kept clean. This is so simple a matter that it should be within the power of the local management to remedy it. A second charge is that the station accommodation is about as bad as it could well be. There is in point of fact no accommodation whatever. A third charge is that no one knows at what hour trains will start from or arrive at any point on the

The pride of the Victoria and Sidney was 2-6-0 No. 1. The husky locomotive was built by the Canadian Locomotive Company for the line in 1893. This station scene shows No. 1 with the *Cordwood Limited* at Sidney. — Provincial Archives

The V&S always seemed to be in trouble. On one occasion a combine rolled off the end of the Sidney wharf and had to be towed around to Bazan Bay for recovery. Here, a work crew with No. 3 begins the long process of getting the passenger car out of the surf and back onto the tracks. (BELOW) A tender full of cordwood did not last long so the crews made sure to pile as much on as possible. In this scene, locomotive No. 1 is shown with the daily mixed train at Victoria. — Both Provincial Archives

road. An hour of departure is fixed for Victoria and Sidney, but on the majority of occasions it is treated as a matter of absolute indifference. A fourth charge is that the delays along the line are intolerable. There surely can be no necessity for the public to put up with this state of things. The direct loss to the people of the Saanich Peninsula is large; the inconvenience to them is very great. The development of the whole peninsula is retarded by the execrable service.

Something must be done. The Victoria Board of Trade ought to take the matter up. The City Council, which pays its share of the interest regularly should assert itself. The Provincial Government ought to take any steps that may be open to it to compel the company to do its duty to the public. We do not know whether the Railway Commission has any powers that can be exerted in the premises, but if it has they also should be called into effect.

The Great Northern Railway company is pursuing an exceedingly foolish policy in connection with this railway. That company may at some time have occasion to ask the people of Victoria for consideration, and we can assure it that if it irritates the public much more it will find itself utterly out of court.

In 1910, the company abandoned its Cormorant Street station in the Market Building and moved the end of track up to Blanchard Street, a few

At the Market Building Station, the farthest extension into Victoria of the V&S, passengers await the departure of the morning train to Sidney. — PROVINCIAL ARCHIVES (BELOW) Great Northern 4-4-0 No. 290 was loaned to the V&S by its parent company near the end of operations on the ill-fated little railway. When it became apparent that nothing could save the V&S, Great Northern equipment was withdrawn and assigned to work on the mainland. — NORMAN GIDNEY COLLECTION

blocks away. This eliminated the necessity of bringing the trains through the city business district.

In 1913, competition for the V&S appeared when the British Columbia Electric Railway Company built an interurban railroad to Deep Bay (now Deep Cove) in North Saanich, supplementing its well established streetcar lines in the City of Victoria. The new interurban offered a more frequent and continuous passenger service than could be provided with existing equipment by the V&S. In addition, with the scheduling of two freight trains a day to Deep Cove, the interurban competed favorably for the shipment of local produce and freight to and from Victoria. To improve the operation of its little subsidiary, the Great Northern supplied the V&S with a modern, well-equipped gas-electric passenger coach which provided passenger accommodations comparable to the B. C. Electric's interurbans and freed an additional locomotive for the hauling of freight.

Gas car No. 2301 of the Great Northern Railway was transferred to operate on the V&S in 1913 to meet the competition of the newly completed B.C. Electric interurban. — H. J. BROWN COLLECTION

Business on the V&S briefly picked up, and the competition between the two lines was intense. Four years after the establishment of the B.C. Electric service on the Saanich Peninsula, the Canadian Northern Pacific Railway also began a passenger service on its new Patricia Bay subdivision. With competition from two other railroads, the Victoria and Sidney Railway could not be kept on a paying basis. Two bad winters had caused long delays in traffic and had further deteriorated the poorly maintained right-of-way. Finally, late in 1917, when the original mortgage came due for payment, the Great Northern Railway removed all of the equipment it had loaned to the V&S. The old equipment provided a vestige of service until April 1919, when the Victoria and Sidney Railway was officially abandoned. Later, Canadian National Railways, having taken over the Canadian Northern Pacific, purchased the section of V&S track connecting its Patricia Bay line to Sidney so that it could receive freight and lumber shipments from the town. In 1935, the Canadian National Railways' line was itself abandoned, and rail connection between Victoria and Sidney was completely severed.

Victoria, shown in this scene from the 1890's, was the site of the first street railway operations in western Canada. — VANCOUVER PUBLIC LIBRARY

The long history of streetcar and interurban service in Victoria and on the Saanich Peninsula began in late 1888, when the National Electric Tramway and Light Company reached agreement with the City of Victoria to operate a number of streetcar routes within the city limits. In September 1889, a contract was let to Messrs. Lyne and Mile for construction of a carbarn and power house at the corner of Constance and Store Streets. Two months later the first streetcars arrived in Victoria from the firm of Patterson and Corbin of St. Catharines, Ontario. These first cars were small 16-foot four-wheeled coaches. Each had an official capacity of 60 to 70 people, although this many passengers in such a small car could not have been very comfortable.

Initially only two short lines were built. One extended from Store Street, along Johnson and Fort Streets to the Royal Jubilee Hospital at Fort and Richmond. The second ran from the corner of Douglas Street and Hillside Avenue to the Outer Wharf near Ogden Point. On completion of the construction work, the system was formally opened on February 27, 1890, at 1:30 P.M. by British Columbia's Lieutenant Governor Nelson. The four streetcars of the National Electric Tramway and Light Company were all gaily decorated for the occasion and carried full loads of dignitaries and

National Electric Tramway and Light Company's No. 5 was typical of the first streetcars operated in Victoria. When first placed in service, these cars lacked even the sophistication of having windshields to protect the motormen. — PROVINCIAL ARCHIVES

guests over the entire four miles of track in the system. Victorians had cause to celebrate, for at the time only two other cities in all of Canada, namely Windsor and St. Catharines in Ontario, had electric street railways.

In 1890, under provincial charter, the company obtained wider operating licenses which enabled it to build lines into the unincorporated districts surrounding the city. The streetcar lines were quickly extended to other parts of the Greater Victoria area. By 1891, 11 cars were in operation on 12 miles of track. The new streetcar system was not without problems, however. In 1892, fire destroyed the company's power house which, in addition to serving the streetcars, supplied electricity to the city. While the power house was being rebuilt, it was necessary to stop running the streetcars at 4:00 P.M. because this was a peak period of domestic power consumption. In January of the following year, the company's Edison generator broke down, leaving streetcars stranded all over the city. Crews were sent out with teams of horses to bring back the immobilized cars.

In 1894 the streetcar system was reincorporated under the name, Victoria Electric Railway and Light Company. However, because of a nationwide depression, this company was soon forced into bankruptcy. It was sold under foreclosure on April 11, 1896, to British interests, which had also acquired the Vancouver Electric Railway and Light Company and the Westminster and Vancouver Tramway Company operating on the mainland of British Columbia. The new firm was known as the Consolidated Railway and Light Company. Much of the credit for the establishment of this new company went to a young English financier,

When the streetcar line to Esquimalt was opened in 1890, it was called an interurban for reasons that are evident in this illustration. This scene shows one of the small single-truck cars clattering over a short trestle beside the main road between Victoria and the naval base at Esquimalt.—PROVINCIAL ARCHIVES

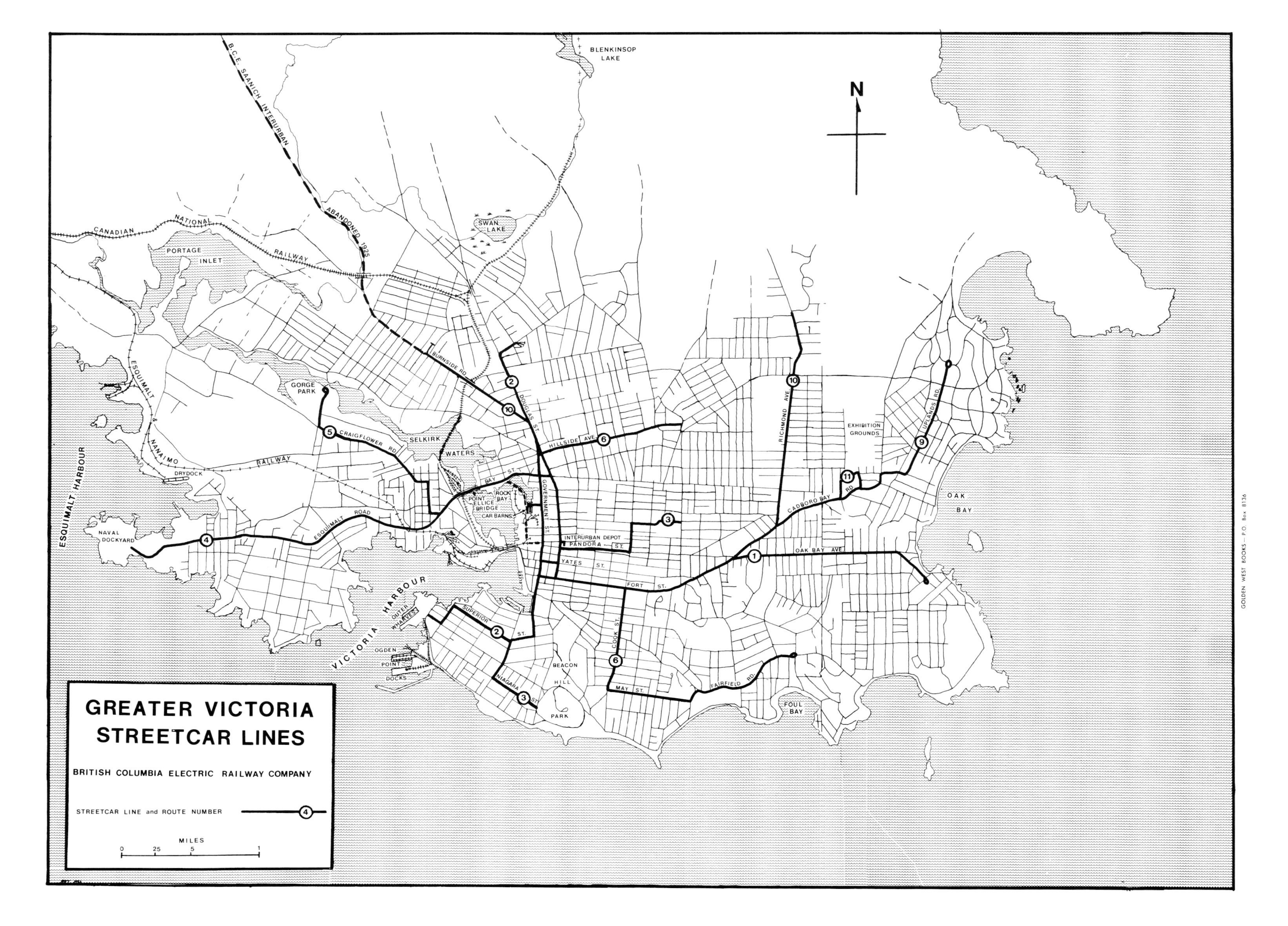
GREATER VICTORIA
STREETCAR LINES
BRITISH COLUMBIA ELECTRIC RAILWAY COMPANY
STREETCAR LINE and ROUTE NUMBER
MILES
0
.25
.5
1
N
BLENKINSOP LAKE
B.C.E. SAANICH INTERURBAN
ABANDONED 1925
CANADIAN NATIONAL RAILWAY
SWAN LAKE
PORTAGE INLET
GORGE PARK
ESQUIMALT & NANAIMO RAILWAY
ESQUIMALT HARBOUR
DRYDOCK
NAVAL DOCKYARD
ESQUIMALT ROAD
CRAIGFLOWER RD.
SELKIRK WATERS
BURNSIDE RD.
DOUGLAS ST.
HILLSIDE AVE.
BAY ST.
POINT ELLICE BRIDGE
ROCK BAY
CAR BARNS
GOVERNMENT ST.
INTERURBAN DEPOT
PANDORA ST.
YATES ST.
FORT ST.
VICTORIA HARBOUR
OUTER WHARVES
OGDEN POINT DOCKS
SUPERIOR ST.
NIAGARA ST.
BEACON HILL PARK
COOK ST.
MAY ST.
FAIRFIELD RD.
FOUL BAY
OAK BAY AVE.
CADBORO BAY RD.
RICHMOND AVE.
EXHIBITION GROUNDS
UPLANDS RD.
OAK BAY
GOLDEN WEST BOOKS — P.O. Box 8136

Government Street in Victoria is one of the main north-south routes through the business district. In the early 1890's, when this scene was photographed, it featured wooden sidewalks, but the street was as yet unpaved. Here, one of the system's 11 cars passes a funeral procession as passersby pause to watch. — PROVINCIAL ARCHIVES

Robert Horne-Payne, who succeeded in convincing enough investors in England of the promise and potential of the electric companies in British Columbia.

On May 26, 1896, just as the success of the new company seemed assured, a tragic accident occurred which led to its collapse. A streetcar overloaded with about 120 people on their way to the Victoria Day holiday celebrations at Esquimalt was rumbling across the Point Ellice Bridge when one of the center spans collapsed. The ten ton car plunged into Victoria Harbour, carrying with it two carriages, a bicyclist, several pedestrians, and a small boat which it crushed below the bridge. Fifty-four people lost their lives in the disaster and many others were injured. The gay holiday became a day of mourning. The news was reported all over the United States and Canada, and eventually reached the backers of the company — the Railway Amalgamation Syndicate — who withdrew their support for Horne-Payne's enterprise. The Consolidated Railway and Light Company was unable to meet its financial obligations and was taken over by the bondholders and sold at auction in October of the same year.

It later developed that the City of Victoria, which owned the faulty bridge, and not the Consolidated Railway and Light Company, was responsible for the tragedy. Horne-Payne and his close associate, Frank Barnard, succeeded in raising further British capital and were able to buy out Consolidated Railway and Light Company's assets at the auction for $2,250,000. On April 3, 1897, the British Columbia Electric Railway Com-

Streetcar No. 14 operated on the Fort and Douglas Street line. (BELOW) Tragedy struck Victoria and ruined the Consolidated Railway and Light Company when, on May 26, 1896, the Esquimalt car fell through the Point Ellice Bridge. Fifty-four people died and many more were injured. — BOTH PROVINCIAL ARCHIVES

The intersection of Douglas and Yates was quiet and uncrowded on this sunny afternoon in the 1890's. The only vehicles were two streetcars and one buggy. On the City Hall clock in the background, the time is 2:40. — Provincial Archives

pany was formed from these assets. Horne-Payne became Chairman of the Board of Directors and Barnard was elected Managing Director.

By the turn of the century, 14 miles of streetcar line were in operation in Victoria, with 20 cars providing an increasingly popular service to the city residents. Fares were based on three types of passages. "Unlimited" fares, for which green tickets were issued, were good on all lines any time of the day and could be bought at six for a quarter. "Limited" fares, with white tickets could be used only between 6:00 and 8:00 A.M. and between 5:00 and 7:00 P.M. during weekdays. These sold at eight for a quarter. School children were given a special reduction of eight fares for a quarter between 8:00 A.M. and 5:00 P.M. on weekdays. Transfers could be made to the Esquimalt line for an additional charge of five cents.

The streetcar company was in constant dispute with the city over the bridging of Victoria's Inner Harbour. For many years cars on the Esquimalt run had been limited to small 7.5-ton vehicles because of the antiquated wooden bridge across Rock Bay between Store and Bridge Streets. Residents began to complain about the quality of the Esquimalt service, but the company contended that it could do nothing until the city rebuilt the Rock Bay Bridge to accommodate 30-ton cars. The city refused to make the needed expenditures and the argument continued over many years. To make matters worse, the damaged Point Ellice Bridge was not fully rebuilt until 1903, so that the size of streetcars was limited on that structure as well.

At Government and Fort Streets, the Beacon Hill Park car stops momentarily to let two passengers board. — Provincial Archives

Most Victoria residents sided with the streetcar company in the dispute with the city, especially after the company, with an understanding that the Rock Bay Bridge would be rebuilt, ordered three new cars for the Esquimalt line from the Ottawa Car and Foundry Company. The new cars arrived late in March 1901, being shipped to Ladysmith by ferry and brought to Victoria over the Esquimalt and Nanaimo Railway. They were the most modern available and cost the company nearly $20,000. The electrical equipment for the cars was furnished by Westinghouse Electric Company. Their trucks were the latest Brill Type 27. Inside, they were fitted with upholstered oak seats, reading lights, and electric push-buttons for calling the conductor. As an added feature, a separate smoking compartment was provided. For safety, a new fender, invented by the company's Thomas Watson, was fitted to both ends of each car. Even after these cars arrived, no work was done on the bridges. Placed in operation on May 3, 1901, the new equipment was used on the Fort Street line for just over a week, but then the company decided to send one of the new cars and an older Victoria car to Vancouver, as it saw no hope of being able to use the new equipment on the Esquimalt run as was originally intended. The people of Victoria were bitterly disappointed.

Riding Victoria's streetcars could be both eventful and exciting. It was possible for the unwary traveller to get a severe jolt from the early electrical equipment, and seasickness was not uncommon. Cars often failed to stop for passengers, merely slowed slightly for the more agile to jump on and off. The Esquimalt line in particular was famous for its lively crowds of sailors returning to the navy base at the end of the line. Derailments were frequent and it was not uncommon for the sailors to scramble out, joking and cheering, and lift the car bodily back onto the tracks. Cows sleeping on the tracks, dust and mud also contributed to the character of these early operations.

In 1901, the British Columbia Electric Railway Company began the construction of larger, more up-to-date carbarns at the corner of Pembroke

In the 1890's, the Esquimalt line ended outside St. Paul's Garrison Church. In later years, as the naval facilities at Esquimalt expanded and as guns were installed on Signal Hill to protect the entrance to Esquimalt Harbour, the church was moved to its pres ent site about one mile closer to Victoria. To avo shattering the windows in the streetcars, the gunners had to make sure the car had left the terminal before firing the battery's 9.2-inch guns. — Provincial Archives

Open cars like No. 20 on the left were very popular in the summer months, being used in regular service and for special sightseeing trips. The demand for this type of car ultimately led to the construction of the larger observation cars shown on the following page. (BELOW) No. 23 and the identical No. 22 were built by Ottawa Car and Foundry for the Esquimalt line in 1901 but were used only on the Fort Street and Oak Bay Beach run because of weight restrictions on the bridges over Victoria Harbour. — BOTH PROVINCIAL ARCHIVES

and Store Streets in order to service the growing number of streetcars used in Victoria. Over the next few years the lines were extended, and in many cases double-tracked. The troublesome route over Rock Bay was at last eliminated by new tracks on Bay and Government Streets, making it possible to use heavier equipment on the Esquimalt line. One of the most impressive additions to the streetcar system was a line constructed through Esquimalt to the Gorge and the beautiful Gorge Park, complete with picnic facilities and Japanese Tea Gardens, which was opened in May 1905. For years Gorge Park remained a popular center for public picnics, swimming parties, and excursions. Most of the park's visitors travelled there by streetcar, and thus the company was more than repaid for its investment.

Open observation cars were introduced into the city service in the early 1900's and became extremely popular during the spring and summer months. Often used on the Oak Bay line, they were sometimes called "Golfers' Specials." They were also frequently used on sightseeing tours of the city. Unlike the standard coaches, in which seats ran the length of the coach, separated by a passage way, these cars had seats extending from side to side with no center aisle. A narrow running board on either side of the car was provided for the conductor to collect fares and for passenger boarding.

The B.C. Electric operations in Victoria, Vancouver, and the lower mainland of the province had grown to such proportions that the company soon began manufacturing nearly all of its own equipment and rolling stock. In some cases, however, orders exceeded the production capacity of the shops. For example, in 1909, the crews were engaged in building 16 passenger cars and an observation car for Vancouver, six cars and a locomotive for New Westminster, 12 cars and two locomotives for the mainland interurbans, and an observation car and several coaches for Victoria. As a result, other equipment needed by the lines had to be ordered from the East.

At the turn of the century, many of Victoria's streets were still unpaved, and residents were forced to tolerate thick mud in the winter and clouds of dust in the summer. To alleviate the dust problem, the company acquired a water car for street sprinkling in the spring of 1906, to be placed in service throughout the dry summer months.

In 1909, the B. C. Electric ordered its first single ended cars for use in Victoria. Since turning loops were available only on the Oak Bay and Willows lines, the use of the cars was initially confined to these runs. They were the largest cars used in Victoria to that date. With them, it was no longer necessary for the operator to remove the controller and air brake handles and place them in position at the other end of the car and then change the trolley poles around at the end of each trip. In order to derive maximum benefit from the new one-ended cars, numerous alterations and additions to existing routes were made.

By the early 1900's Victoria had grown to be a modern bustling city with paved streets, concrete sidewalks, and of course, an up-to-date street railway system. This scene shows the corner of Government Street and Broughton Street. — Provincial Archives

In the same year, the new observation car, completed in the busy company shops, finally arrived at Victoria. It was an entirely open car, with seats arranged in tiers rising towards the back of the car, so that each rider had an unobstructed view. The car was ideal for summer tourists, who took full advantage of it for sightseeing throughout the city. It proved very popular and received widespread advertising in tourist publications and in books encouraging settlement in the district.

To keep up with the increasing demand for electricity, the B.C. Electric Railway Company began work on a large hydro-electric plant at Jordan River, and plans were formalized for a major expansion of the electric railway system. For many years, the idea of building an electric railway line through the Saanich Peninsula had been discussed with growing interest in Victoria, particularly in view of the badly deteriorating service on the Victoria and Sidney Railway's line. In 1910, a pro-

In 1909, British Columbia Electric Railway Company shop crews in Vancouver constructed two spacious observation cars. No. 123 was assigned to Victoria and was an immediate success. The car was used on trips through Esquimalt and to Oak Bay and Gorge Park. For a time it was operated regularly on the No. 5 route to the Gorge. However, the car was eventually transferred to Vancouver where longer more heavily patronized runs could be operated. — Provincial Archives

In the scene on the left, track crews are busy laying tracks into the depot of the new Saanich interurban line at the corner of Douglas and Pandora in downtown Victoria. Initial operations began in July 1912 and the line was in full service by June of the following year. — PROVINCIAL ARCHIVES

Electric locomotive No. 981, shown at the left, and No. 951 were used in freight and maintenance service on the Saanich line. — NORMAN GIDNEY (BELOW) The opening of the new interurban on June 13, 1913 saw a specially decorated train operate from Victoria to Deep Bay. In this view, the brightly polished cars pause at one of the small shelters built along the line. — VICTORIA PRESS COLLECTION

posal to build an interurban railroad from Victoria 24 miles north to the end of the Saanich Peninsula was officially put forward. The idea was favorably received, and work was soon begun to survey and grade the right-of-way. In March 1912, a temporary service was initiated along Burnside Road to the city limits at Harriet Road on the first completed section of the interurban line.

By July, grading of the entire right-of-way was nearly completed. Because of previous agreements between the village of Sidney and the Victoria and Sidney Railway Company, the Saanich Interurban was denied access to the village. Instead, the northern terminus was located to the west at Deep Bay, now known as Deep Cove. The route ran west of the Victoria and Sidney Railway and served a number of small settlements some distance away from the V&S line. At Saanichton, the routes ran together and paralleled each other for about a mile before diverging at Bazan Bay.

As track laying progressed on the interurban, a connecting track was built between the two railroads, and the V&S found itself delivering cars and equipment to its future competitor. Early in June 1913, two interurban cars were brought over the V&S from Sidney to Saanichton, and on the 18th of the month, with the line completed, official opening ceremonies took place. Sir Richard McBride, Premier of British Columbia, drove the last spike to commemorate the event. Service was established immediately, with six return trips a day to the end of the line. Fares were based on a three cent per mile rate, and there was no reduction for return trips. Children rode for half the adult fare. Shortly, the service was expanded further, with eleven return passenger runs and two freight trains a day scheduled. The interurban was a serious threat to business on the Victoria and Sidney Railway, drawing a great deal of traffic that would have otherwise gone to the Great Northern subsidiary.

When the Saanich line began to lose money, the heavy electric interurban equipment was transferred to Vancouver, where it could be operated more profitably. Here, Nos. 1242 and 1241, formerly Saanich line cars, pause at Mead on Vancouver's Central Park line. — C. R. LITTLEBURY PHOTO — NORMAN GIDNEY COLLECTION

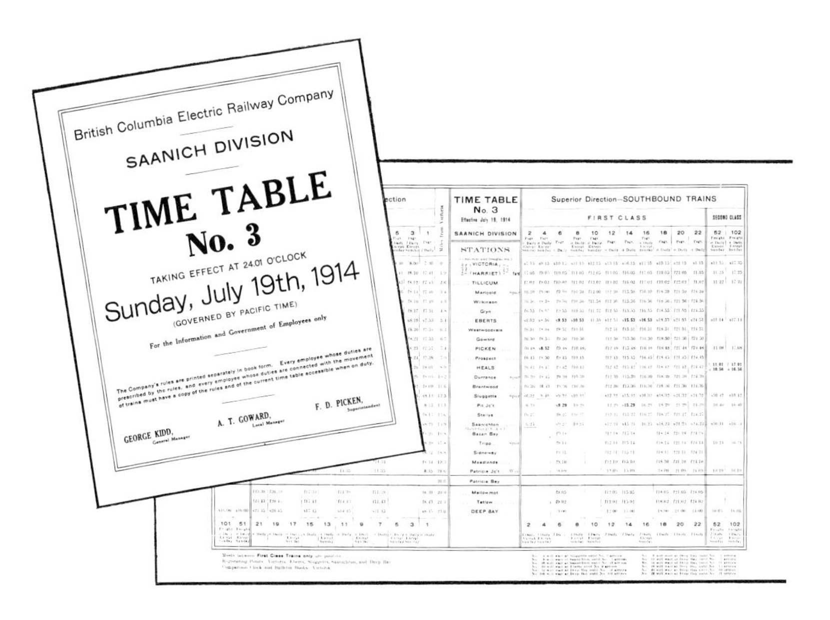

British Columbia Electric Railway Company

SAANICH DIVISION

TIME TABLE
No. 3

TAKING EFFECT AT 24.01 O'CLOCK
Sunday, July 19th, 1914
(GOVERNED BY PACIFIC TIME)

For the Information and Government of Employees only

The Company's rules are printed separately in book form. Every employee whose duties are prescribed by the rules, and every employee whose duties are connected with the movement of trains must have a copy of the rules and of the current time table accessible when on duty.

GEORGE KIDD, General Manager — A. T. GOWARD, Local Manager — F. D. PICKEN, Superintendent

nployees Time Table No. 3 for July 19, 1914 ted two daily-except-Sunday freights in ad- tion to eleven passenger runs in each direc- on over the line. — E. W. BARLOW COLLEC- ON

Meanwhile, business on the city streetcar lines was growing rapidly. In the year 1911 alone, 55 streetcars carried eight and a quarter million riders. The following year was even more successful, with a total of nearly eleven million fares being collected. On the newly opened Burnside line, 36,317 passengers were carried and the new Hillside route accounted for another 45,667 riders. Moreover, at peak times such as Victoria Day, the opening of the racing season, the Victoria Exhibition, and Christmas Eve, fares averaged 40,000 to 50,000 for each day. To accommodate this heavy new patronage, nine new cars and nine other pieces of rolling stock were added to the company's roster. Indeed, 1912 was a good year for the street railway in Victoria.

In January and February of 1916, record snowfalls blanketed Vancouver Island. On February 3, snows combined with a heavy wind caused drifts up to five and six feet, and the City of Victoria was completely paralyzed. Streetcar operations were suspended, and over 30 cars were stranded throughout the city. For several days the downtown area was virtually deserted, as people were unable to get in to work. Soldiers stationed at Willows Camp were called out to help clear the streets. After the streetcars were running again, many derailments occurred. The motor casings on the trucks would ride up onto compacted snow and lift the flanges clear of the rails. As conditions eased, the B.C. Electric made several flatcars available for delivering food and fuel to people in Esquimalt and Oak Bay stranded by the storm. By February 11, the service had been returned to normal and all lines were running on schedule. In appreciation of the soldiers' efforts in clearing the tracks during the storm, the company gave them all free one month passes. The interurban had managed to remain operational throughout the storm by using a snow plow to clear the deeper drifts.

In 1919, the Victoria and Sidney Railway was finally abandoned, due to competition from buses, the B.C. Electric Interurban, and the Canadian Northern Pacific Railway, which had opened a passenger service on its Patricia Bay subdivision. Soon passenger accommodation on this last line was also dropped, and the British Columbia Electric Railway Company was left with a monopoly on rail passenger service on the Saanich Peninsula. However, even this monopoly was not adequate

Record snowfalls in 1916 brought nearly everything to a halt in Victoria. At the height of the storm over 30 streetcars were stranded.—PROVINCIAL ARCHIVES (BELOW) Cars in the 250 series were built in 1911 at the B.C. Electric's shops in Vancouver using steel frames imported from England. — NORMAN GIDNEY

Cars in the 380 series, like No. 387 shown running along Superior Street, were built for the B.C. Electric in 1913 by Preston Car and Coach.—PROVINCIAL ARCHIVES

Two streetcars pass in front of the CPR's impressive Empress Hotel. To the right are the British Columbia Parliment Buildings, and in the background are the Olympic Mountains of Washington State. It is late in the afternoon of a summer day in the 1930's. — PROVINCIAL ARCHIVES

Single truck Birneys like No. 408, built in 1922, were the last new cars acquired for operation in Victoria. With a seating capacity of 32 and room for 20 standees, they were quite adequate for the No. 2 line from Cloverdale to the Outer Wharf. In 1973, No. 400 was placed on display at the Provincial Museum in Victoria after being fully refurbished to like new condition. — NORMAN GIDNEY

to avert the accumulation of a large deficit for the interurban operation. The population of the area was simply too small to support both the rail line and the buses which competed with it. To reduce expenses city streetcars replaced the heavy interurbans, but still the financial position of the line was not improved.

While the interurban struggled on, preparations were underway on all of the British Columbia Electric's lines for changing the rule of the road. In British tradition, traffic had always kept to the left in British Columbia. However, by the early 1920's this situation presented many serious problems when the rest of North America was used to driving on the right. Six o'clock Sunday morning, January 1, 1922 was set as the time when the change to right hand operation would occur. This simple decision carried with it a host of problems for the street railways. Tracks would have to be reconstructed, the overhead wires aligned and many of the cars extensively rebuilt to permit boarding of passengers on the right hand side of the cars. To ease the financial burden on the company, the government subsidized B.C. Electric $370,000 for the changeover.

The company's capable staff had the task well in hand by the end of December 1921. In a statement for the *Times*, the company's general superintendent described the preparations.

So far as is mechanically possible, we have everything ready for the change in the rule of the road.

Although we have been very busy for the past few months getting our preparations completed to the actual point where the change must be definitely made, and have had some hundred additional skilled mechanics working on the alterations to the rolling stock, yet there is a phase of the work which cannot be done until the actual reversal of traffic takes place.

When the cars begin to come into the sheds on the evening of December 31, is the time we shall experience the peak of our labors. Until then we can only go on making preparations, perfecting our plans and organization for dealing with the situation before us.

As each car comes off the run on Saturday night, it will be taken to the barns where a gang of mechanics will be waiting to receive it and complete the finishing touches under the right-hand rule.

This means that all temporary air lines, electric cables, etc., which have made it possible to operate the cars in a partially completed condition, will have to be removed and the permanent connections installed in their place.

It will be necessary to send out a few cars with the seats facing backwards for several days after the

When this photo of No. 22 was taken in September 1940, the beautifully maintained coach was nearly 40 years old. Nos. 22 and 23 saw a variety of service on the Victoria street railway system before being retired in the mid-1940's. They ran on the Saanich interurban line, and were used as snowplows, and finally ended their days as the regular cars on the No. 10 line on Burnside Road. These cars are remembered as the sturdiest, and the most comfortable on the system. — NORMAN GIDNEY

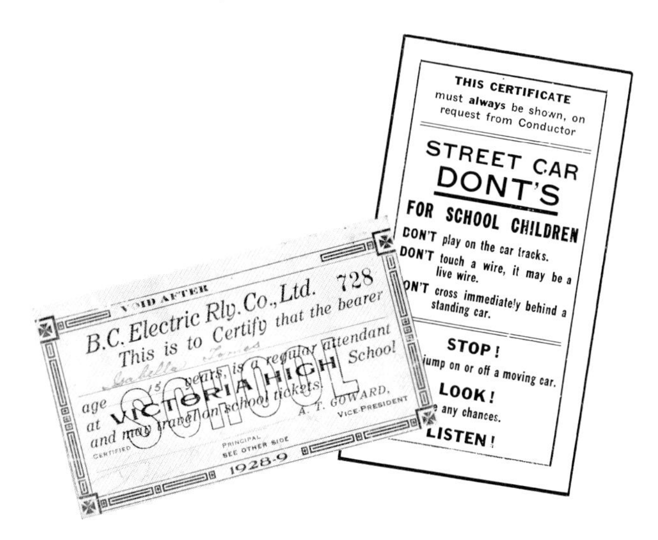
THIS CERTIFICATE must always be shown, on request from Conductor

STREET CAR DONT'S FOR SCHOOL CHILDREN

DON'T play on the car tracks.
DON'T touch a wire, it may be a live wire.
DON'T cross immediately behind a standing car.

STOP! jump on or off a moving car.
LOOK! any chances.
LISTEN!

VOID AFTER
B.C. Electric Rly. Co., Ltd. 728
This is to Certify that the bearer
age 15 years, is a regular attendant
at VICTORIA HIGH School
and may travel on school tickets.
A. T. GOWARD, VICE-PRESIDENT
SCHOOL
CERTIFIED PRINCIPAL SEE OTHER SIDE
1928-9

change, but these will be taken into the shops and completed as fast as we can handle them. There are a number of double-ended cars which have not yet been converted. These cars will be used for temporary right-hand operation and will be changed as soon as possible to conform with the new rule of the road. . . .

With regard to the track and overhead trolley, there is still a considerable amount of work to be done — switches to be changed, points to be reset, cross-overs to be changed, etc., but we are in a position to operate under the right-hand rule at the present time and the balance of the work, which will be of a permanent nature, will be carried out as expeditiously as possible. . . . We have practically doubled our track gang and the work is running smoothly and satisfactorily.

The final moment arrived and the changeover proceeded without incident. To further change the traditional procedures of the street railway, one-man operation of the street cars was instituted on all lines by the summer of 1922. Meanwhile, the financial position of the Saanich interurban continued to deteriorate. Even one-man operation on the line did not help in cutting the losses. The decision to abandon the interurban was reached in September 1924, and service was discontinued the following month. In July 1925, the tracks were torn up north of the city limits at Harriet Street

The No. 10 line ran from Richmond Avenue via Fort Street through downtown Victoria and along Douglas to Burnside, where it terminated at the corner of Carroll Street. (RIGHT) Here a large number of passengers would frequently be waiting to board the trolleys. — AUTHOR'S COLLECTION (BELOW) Less than ten years after the photograph at the right was taken, the street railway era in Victoria ended as No. 383 made the last run from Beacon Hill Park to the carbarn on June 5, 1948. In this view, the last car passes the Empress Hotel. — PROVINCIAL ARCHIVES

and the cars were assigned to service elsewhere in the city. By this time, 62 streetcars and a variety of miscellaneous equipment were in operation on 41 miles of track around Greater Victoria. However, automobiles were beginning to draw more and more people away from the streetcars, and the economy of bus operation was becoming obvious.

A preview of the future public transit system for Victoria came in the fall of 1928, when the B.C. Electric took delivery of 23 new buses for city service. The basic street railway system remained unchanged from the operations of the 1920's for two more decades. Buses were operated in conjunction with the streetcars, serving alternate routes and outlying districts. After World War II the company began phasing out its street railways, even in downtown Victoria.

By the spring of 1948, the rails to Esquimalt had been removed, and the Esquimalt and Nanaimo Railway had taken over some of the streetcar tracks near its yards. A number of the old cars were sold for diners and summer homes, and two single truck Birney streetcars were sold for $100 each and trucked out to the Goldstream Hotel, where they remained for a number of years. Others were towed away and burned at the Esquimalt and Nanaimo Railway yards.

On June 5, 1948, the last streetcar run was made with appropriate ceremony. Car No. 383 was run out to the end of the Beacon Hill line. There, civic dignitaries, Chamber of Commerce directors and company officials boarded the car for a last run through Victoria. The following day, the roar of buses had forever replaced the sparking and clanging of the old streetcars in Victoria.

The construction of the water pipeline from Sooke Lake to Victoria between 1913 and 1915 resulted in the operation of one of the most makeshift railroads on Vancouver Island. Power for the 2-foot gauge line was provided by the Davenport 0-4-0T shown on the right. The jack on the front of the locomotive indicates that the crew had difficulties keeping the little teakettle on the tracks. — MRS. G. HODGESON COLLECTION

Pipe for the water system, shown at the right, was fabricated at a yard near Cooper's Cove. (BELOW) The little Davenport locomotive steams across the unbelievably fragile-looking trestle at "East Bend." A completed section of the pipeline is visible behind the trestle. The locomotive was typical of machines used on construction projects for moving fill and building materials. After this job was completed in 1915, the locomotive was used in a number of large undertakings in southern British Columbia. — BOTH MRS. G. HODGESON COLLECTION

During the building of the government drydock at Esquimalt in the early 1920's, the Pacific Construction Company employed a small railroad to facilitate the huge excavation. The operation used five locomotives, three steam shovels and 45 dump cars. When completed, the drydock was one of the largest in the world. It has berthed such giant ships as the Cunard Line's *Queen Elizabeth* during the Second World War.—VANCOUVER PUBLIC LIBRARY

Although the tracks and equipment of the three railroads on the Saanich Peninsula disappeared long ago, interested observers can still trace the paths taken by the trains, and, with a little imagination, can picture the railroads as they must have been half a century ago.

The right-of-way of the Patricia Bay subdivision of the Canadian Northern Pacific Railway (later Canadian National Railways) is now partly a roadway, Lochside Drive, portions of which extend from Mackenzie Avenue along the east coast of the peninsula to Sidney. Large sections remain unused, except as bridle trails and footpaths. In places the original wooden ties can be found, and at Blenkinsop Lake, close to Mackenzie Avenue, the footings of a large trestle which once spanned the lake can still be seen.

The Victoria and Sidney Railway, routed through the center of the Saanich Peninsula, is also discernible in many places. The built up grade can be seen along Glanford Avenue, and Pipeline Road in Royal Oak was once a part of the line. Further north, a trail follows the right-of-way along the western shore of Elk Lake. In Central Saanich the line is commemorated as Veyaness Road ("V. an' S."). The Prairie Inn, still standing at the corner of Mount Newton Cross Road and East Saanich Road, was a frequent stop of the old "Cordwood Limited."

The right-of-way of the Saanich Interurban, along the western side of the peninsula, now forms Interurban Road and, in Central Saanich, Wallace Drive. North of the Patricia Bay Airport, Tatlow Road follows the route to Deep Cove. In Victoria, the B.C. Electric's carbarns at Pembroke and Store Streets stand little changed from when they were built at the turn of the century. Gorge Park, which for some time was neglected and little used, has been beautifully redeveloped, and is itself a monument to the many years of service given to the people of Victoria by the B.C. Electric streetcars.

In a setting to delight any photographer, CNR 2-8-0 No. 2128 steams along the Tidewater subdivision on its way to Youbou on January 28, 1957. Dieselization was to follow less than two years after this photo was taken.—DAVE WILKIE

4

CANADIAN NATIONAL RAILWAYS

CANADIAN National Railways' lines on Vancouver Island were originally part of the short-lived Canadian Northern Pacific Railway, the western extension into British Columbia of the Canadian Northern Railway built across the Canadian prairies by railroad promoters William Mackenzie and Donald Mann. After the rails reached Edmonton, Alberta, in 1905, survey parties were sent into the Rockies and Coast Ranges of British Columbia to locate the right-of-way to the Pacific. By 1909, a route had been selected penetrating the Rockies by way of Yellowhead Pass, traversing what is now Jasper National Park, and following the Fraser and Thompson rivers through the interior of British Columbia to the Fraser's mouth at Port Mann near Vancouver. In March 1910, the Canadian Northern Pacific Railway was incorporated, and with the aid of grants from the Provincial Government, construction work began in that year.

Extensions were also proposed for Vancouver Island, to run from Victoria, at the southern tip of the Island, west and north through extensive stands of Douglas fir, cedar, and hemlock to Port Alberni at the head of a west coast inlet. From there, routes north to Campbell River and then west along the Gold River to Muchalet Inlet were also surveyed.

On February 18, 1911, this line was dedicated and work began on the grade from Victoria to Port Alberni. Contracts for the first 100 miles of construction were awarded. Grant, Smith and Company were to undertake the work for 60 miles north of Victoria, while Messrs. Moore and Pethick were to clear and grade an additional 40 miles of right-of-way to the western end of Cowichan Lake. Beyond Cowichan Lake, the right-of-way to the west coast passed through the dense Pacific rain forests, which according to some form the most impenetrable jungles in the world. The salal shrubs and other underbrush are often 12 to 15 feet high. Needless to say, the early engineering crews were faced with a difficult task indeed.

Lawrence Macrae, one of the engineers on the survey parties, recalls that out of a crew of 22 men, starting on a three month expedition into the Coleman Creek area west of Cowichan Lake, only three were able to cope with the salal and the steady drizzle of rain long enough to finish the job. Many times the men were forced to move all of their material by dugout canoe or by pulling rafts down the icy creeks which cut through the forests to Alberni Inlet. On one occasion, a crew member wandered off the trail and soon became lost in the thick undergrowth. His companions searched vainly for him but were forced to aban-

Past Cowichan Lake and along Alberni Inlet, grading crews built the right-of-way for the CNR. However, the tracks were never laid into Port Alberni as was originally intended. In these scenes, excavation and rock work is proceeding through the dense rain forests northwest of Nitinat Lake. — BOTH VANCOUVER PUBLIC LIBRARY

don their rescue attempt, hoping that he could make it back by himself. Three days later, he stumbled into camp, hungry and exhausted, but alive. He had managed to work his way down to the coast and then back along Coleman Creek to camp. Luckily for him, the huckleberries were in season.

While surveying and grading continued on the Victoria to Alberni line, work began on a shorter section of right-of-way running north from Victoria through the rolling agricultural lands of the Saanich Peninsula to the sheltered harbour of Patricia Bay. This 16-mile line was to serve as a connection for ferry service to the mainland operations of the Canadian Northern Pacific at Port Mann. It was also designed to compete with the Victoria Terminal Railway and Ferry Company for through freight and passenger business to the lower mainland.

A ferry terminal was built at Patricia Bay, with the dock extending 2,200 feet out over the shallow tidal mud flats to deep water where barges could be safely unloaded. Two tugs and two barges, each capable of carrying eight railway cars, were built for the service at Port Mann. In addition, a large steam powered car ferry equipped with passenger accommodations was ordered from the Davie Shipbuilding and Repairing Company at Luzon, Quebec, to provide a fast daily service to Vancouver Island. Grading for the Patricia Bay subdivision was completed 13 months after work began in October 1913. Because of the shortage of rail, imposed by the demands of the escalating war in Europe, it was not until April 9, 1916, that the first Canadian Northern Pacific locomotive, 2-6-0 No. 105, arrived in Victoria. Total cost for the Patricia Bay line was $1,180,000. Grades were moderate, with a maximum of only 1.1 percent, and the curves were kept to a minimum for the entire route.

A temporary terminus was built just inside the city limits of Victoria at Alpha Street pending the completion of a road overpass and a long pile trestle and bridge over the Selkirk Waters separating the Saanich Peninsula from the railroad's terminal site in Victoria West. The line was opened

CANADIAN NORTHERN PACIFIC RAILWAY
(Patricia Bay Line)

GAS-ELECTRIC MOTOR CAR SERVICE

EFFECTIVE APRIL 30TH, 1917

COLONIST PRESSES

[C]ADIAN NORTHERN PACIFIC RAILWAY
(PATRICIA BAY LINE)
GAS-ELECTRIC MOTOR CAR SERVICE
Effective April 30th, 1917

[Daily] Except [Sunday]	Daily Except Sunday	Mileage	STATIONS	Mileage	Daily Except Sunday	Daily Except Sunday
[8.3]0 A.M.	Lv. 5.15 P.M.	1.23	VICTORIA (Alpha Street)	0.00	Ar. 10.45 A.M.	Ar. 7.30 P.M.
[8.]39 "	5.24 "	1.82	JUNCTION	1.10	10.36 "	7.21 "
[8.]44 "	5.29 "		NORTH QUADRA	4.77	10.31 "	7.16 "
[8].55 "	5.40 "		CORDOVA	5.60	10.20 "	7.05 "
8.58 "	5.43 "		SAYWARD	8.00	10.17 "	7.02 "
9.05 "	5.50 "		MARTINDALE	8.82	10.10 "	6.55 "
9.09 "	5.54 "		MICHELL	10.33	10.06 "	6.51 "
9.12 "	5.57 "		SAANICH	10.64	10.03 "	6.48 "
9.14 "	5.59 "		SCOTT	12.66	10.01 "	6.46 "
9.17 "	6.02 "		BAZAN	13.61	9.58 "	6.43 "
9.20 "	6.05 "		EAST ROAD	14.27	9.55 "	6.40 "
9.24 "	6.09 "		RANGE ROAD	15.10	9.51 "	6.36 "
Ar. 9.30 "	Ar. 6.15 "		PATRICIA BAY	15.33	Lv. 9.45 "	Lv. 6.30 "
			Transfer [illegible]			

Competition from buses and two other rail lines led to losses on the CNP line to Patricia Bay. The schedule, on the left, shows the service provided when the line was opened. — E. W. BARLOW COLLECTION

by the CNP's district engineer D. O. Lewis, and acting assistant general manager, B. T. Chappell, on April 29, 1917. Service was inaugurated the following day, with a 74 passenger Canadian General Electric gas car of 1912 vintage being placed in operation. The original schedule offered a daily-except-Sunday service with trains leaving Victoria (Alpha Street) at 8:30 A.M. and 5:15 P.M. The return trips left Patricia Bay one hour later. After a short time, a Sunday-only mid-morning train was added to the schedule. Fares were three cents per mile for a one way trip and five cents per mile return.

The line passed through the beach resort areas north of Victoria at Cordova Bay and was very popular in the summer. Workers at the powder manufacturing plant at James Island also found the new service convenient, as it eliminated a long walk from the ferry dock opposite James Island to either the Victoria and Sidney or British Columbia Electric right-of-ways. Competition among the three railroads and the buses or "jitneys" operating on the Saanich Peninsula was intense. Seasonal travellers and the few regular commuters could not provide sufficient patronage to make the new gas car service pay for itself. The company would

Canadian Northern 2-6-0 No. 105 (later renumbered 474 when taken over by the Canadian National) brought the first construction train into Victoria in April 1916. — PROVINCIAL ARCHIVES

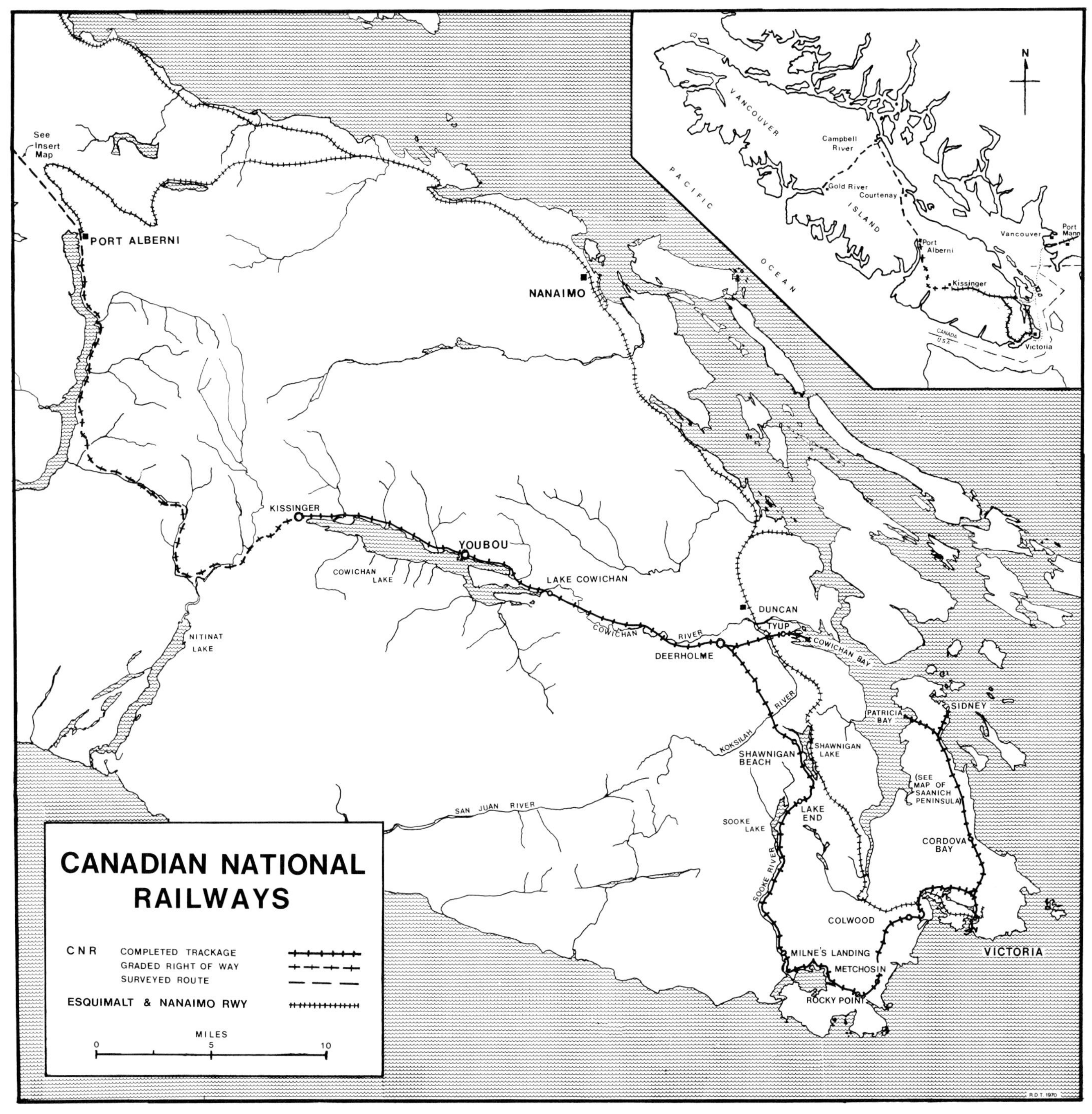

not expand its schedule and risk further deficits without a guarantee of more passengers, and the potential passengers would not use the line because the schedule wasn't convenient. As a result, the gas car service was curtailed early in 1919 after only two years of operation.

Construction on the longer line from Victoria to the west coast of Vancouver Island proceeded slowly throughout the war years. By December 1916, the subgrade had been completed for 137 miles, only 4 miles from Port Alberni. However, the long delays in construction took their toll, as brush gradually took over the right-of-way. The Department of Railways Annual Report pointed out that since the limit of safety for wooden structures was only ten years, even if the line were completed immediately, it would not be long before several of the trestles would have to be renewed. Since there were over two miles of bridging on the railroad, considerable expense would be involved if many of the structures needed replacing.

While the line was very indirect, it possessed a maximum gradient of only 1.5 percent, and this on a total of only 8.8 miles of the route. In addition, it passed through some of the richest timber stands on Vancouver Island, a feature which was to be advantageous to the railroad in later years. However, by the summer of 1918, only four miles of steel had been laid. Becoming impatient, Victoria's Mayor Todd, Premier Oliver, and Dr. Tolmie, Member of Parliament for Victoria, formed a delegation to lobby with the Federal Government in Ottawa for completion of the long delayed railroad. Prompted by a desperate need for spruce for wartime aircraft construction, the Federal Government decided to resume construction of the Canadian Northern Pacific as far as the Nitinat region west of Cowichan Lake, where the coast forests could be tapped. Agreement was reached between the Provincial Government and the Federal authorities for sufficient 60-pound rail to be borrowed from the Pacific Great Eastern Railway to complete the additional trackage.

Amid appropriate ceremony, the line was rededicated on September 9, 1918. The *Victoria Daily Times* described the events in vivid detail.

Gaily decked with bunting, multicolored berries and flowers of every variety, Canadian Northern Railway locomotive No. 1018 (a 4-6-0) left Alpha Street Station promptly at eleven o'clock this morning, and reached the end of steel exactly 40 minutes afterwards. There was no attempt at speed and the four coaches attached to No. 1018 carried the most optimistic "freight" that has ever passed over any British Columbian Railway. Representatives of all Victoria's progressive bodies, legislators, bankers, merchants, transportation officials, representatives of the fair sex, and a heavy leavening of Rotarians made up the party . . . As the train pulled up at the end of steel Premier Oliver who had made his way by automobile, was in readiness in the midst of a goodly crowd . . . A rousing cheer went up from fully four hundred throats as the Premier swung his sledge hammer and struck the first nickel spike squarely on the head. And there was no diminution in the applause until after Dr. Tolmie had followed suit with spike No. 2. Somewhat bashful after the muscular demonstration of the two heavyweights, T. H. White, the Canadian Northern Railway Company's chief engineer, required a little persuasion before he could be induced to try his skill. With no small experience and the "knack" behind him, Mr. White finished a good third and D. O. Lewis, resident engineer for Vancouver Island, completed the official quartet spike driving competition.

Organizer Kingham, however, "spotted" the representatives of the two Services in the persons of Major-General Leckie and Captain Martin and they had perforce to try their skill. To the junior service (the Army) went the plum, and General Leckie demonstrated that he can drive a spike as well as lead a brigade. Captain Martin got away to a bad start and although he finally secured the pin he was obliged to allow for a slant and reverse his overarm action.

Having shown their prowess with the sledge the dignataries began a round of speeches praising the new railroad, the contribution it would make to the war effort and the great progress and development it would bring to Vancouver Island.

Finally it seemed as if the long delayed railroad would at last be completed, but this was not to be. On November 11, 1918, the spruce market collapsed when the Armistice was signed ending World War I. Work continued, but at a much slower pace, as the tracks were gradually extended towards Cowichan Lake.

On December 7 of the same year, the long awaited car ferry arrived from Quebec. The S. S. *Canora* (for CAnadian NOrthern RAilway) steamed into Victoria Harbour at 3:00 in the afternoon. She had completed a 7,444 mile journey, which had taken her from Luzon, Quebec, down the St. Lawrence River to Halifax, where extra coal and a naval cargo for Esquimalt was loaded, and eventually through the Panama Canal to Victoria. The ship was of steel construction, with an overall length of 294 feet and a displacement of 3,400 tons. She was built for operation in both directions, with propellers and steering gear both

The S. S. *Canora* was the Canadian Northern Pacific's answer to the problem of providing fast and reliable connections to its isolated lines on Vancouver Island. — PROVINCIAL ARCHIVES

On October 10, 1922 officials opened the first passenger service on the CN's Cowichan subdivision. Gas car No. 15813, shown on the left at the Point Ellice yards, began the regular schedule three days later. — CANADIAN NATIONAL (BELOW) As the operation was extended and heavier equipment was required, Brill cars like No. 15810 were used on the line. In this scene, the car is shown ready to leave Youbou in the late 1920's. — W. HASANEN

fore and aft, and was capable of 14 knots. Railway cars were accommodated in the enclosed main deck, where three tracks were laid running the length of the vessel.

Reporters commenting on her facilities for passengers were most impressed. "This accommodation includes rooms for all officers, large dining salon, parlour, staterooms for passengers, smoking room, kitchen and pantry, bathroom and lavatories, and a large observation cabin at the forward end. The staterooms will be tastefully finished and have berths, clothes closets, wash basins, etc. in each room." Shortly after her arrival, the *Canora* was taken to Yarrows Limited at Esquimalt for a complete overhaul to prepare her for the coast service. However, before the overhaul could be completed, Canadian Northern Pacific Railway ceased to exist.

On December 20, 1918, a year after the Canadian Government had assumed nominal control over the CNP, Canadian National Railways was formed, and all of the British Columbia operations of the Canadian Northern were absorbed into the nationalized system. The Federal Government felt no compulsion to provide a passenger service from Vancouver Island to the mainland, as Mackenzie and Mann had originally intended. As a result, when the *Canora's* refitting was completed and she was placed in service the following April, only freight was carried between Patricia Bay and Port Mann.

Meanwhile, construction was progressing, although slowly, on the main line to the west coast. By the end of 1919, tracks had reached Mile 52.5, the crossing of the Koksilah River, and by mid-February the canyon had been bridged. The year 1920 also saw the completion of the railway's terminal at Point Ellice in Victoria West. There a five stall engine house was constructed as well as shops, coaling facilities, a water tower, station, and freight shed.

A further addition was made to the Patricia Bay subdivision in 1919 when the Canadian National was granted running rights over a 1.67 mile long section of the Victoria and Sidney Railway shortly after that company had been placed in receivership. Later, after much debate, Canadian National Railways purchased a total of 2.4 miles of V&S track for $25,600, so that freight service could be maintained to the lumber mills and other industries at Sidney.

In August 1922 it was announced that a passenger service would be inaugurated on the Cowichan subdivision from Victoria as far as Sooke. A 30-passenger gas car was brought to Vancouver Island especially for the new service. The car was designed by S. J. Hungerford, Canadian National's vice president for branch line operations, and was built by Ledoux Jennings Limited of Montreal. The No. 15813 was powered by a Reo gasoline engine and was equipped with a small baggage and mail compartment in addition to the 14-foot passenger section. The "train" was operated by one man who served as engineer, conductor, and trainman. On October 10, 1922, the opening trip was

made. A small group of dignitaries was taken to the end of track at Mile 60, where the car was turned and run back to Victoria. On the 13th (a Friday), the first revenue passengers embarked on the first scheduled return trip to Sooke. This car was later replaced by slightly larger Brill rail cars, which remained in service until the end of Canadian National's passenger operations on Vancouver Island.

By the spring of 1924, the tracks had finally reached the east end of Cowichan Lake, 73 miles from Victoria, and work was progressing on a ten mile extension along the north shore of the lake to the town of Youbou. The completion of the Canadian National Railways' line into the Cowichan Lake area had a tremendous impact on the logging industry. Within one year of the opening of this section of line, five new timber companies had established logging operations connecting with the main line of the CNR. In a feature article, the *Victoria Daily Times* listed the companies operating along the line: "The Echo Logging Company at Sooke Lake, Napier Logging Company at Mile 51, the Copeland Logging Company at Mile 53, the National Pacific Logging Company at Mile 56, Ferguson Bros. at Deerholme and the Deerholme Logging Company near the same location, Cameron Logging Company at Mile 54

While Consolidations dominated the roster of the CN on Vancouver Island in the later years of steam, Ten-Wheelers could be seen on the majority of freight runs during the 1920's. No. 1451, shown above, switching the car ferry at Point Ellice in July 1956, was a late arrival on the Cowichan subdivision. — Stan F. Styles

Outside the Point Ellice shops three Moguls, Nos. 411, 424, and 426, and two Consolidations, Nos. 2116 and 2110, crowd the engine terminal in this April 1938 scene. — Dave Wilkie

and 70, the Scottish Logging Company at Mile 65, and the Channel Logging Company at Miles 69, 71, and 73."

After the new logging companies had begun operations in the country beyond Shawnigan Lake, the Canadian National decided to extend its passenger service to Mile 69.4 in July 1923. By March of the next year, the new line was proving its worth to local residents and businessmen. In addition to the daily passenger service from Victoria, a twice weekly freight train and two or three heavy log trains a day were required to handle the increasing traffic. One large source of freight was the scrap cordwood produced by the mills and used as a domestic fuel in significant quantities until the early 1950's. It was carried in trainloads to Victoria in old boxcars with the roofs removed for easy loading and handling.

Following the completion of the line to Cowichan Lake, lumber and through freight were transported by rail to the ferry dock at Patricia Bay for shipment to the mainland. Because of the low speed restrictions and the 100 mile distance between Cowichan Lake and Patricia Bay, freight costs were high. To eliminate this long haul, the short Tidewater subdivision was built in 1924 from Deerholme at Mile 57.9 on the main line to Cowichan Bay. Here a new ferry slip was built so that traffic to and from Cowichan Lake could be loaded at this point. As a result, the rail haul was reduced to a little over 30 miles, yielding substantial savings in time and money.

Finally in 1928 construction of the Cowichan subdivision ended, 11 miles past Youbou at Kissinger (now known as Nitinat Camp), many miles

The intricate woodwork of the CN's spectacular Koksilah River trestle was a feature of the line that few photographers of the Cowichan subdivision could pass by. Here, No. 2116 rumbles over the structure with a long train of empty flats on October 3, 1946. — JOHN NEWMAN

short of the intended destination of Port Alberni. Plans for further extensions of the line were abandoned, and the grade was left to deteriorate. Before too many years had passed, however, a number of sections of the unfinished right-of-way past Kissinger were utilized by logging firms operating along the Alberni Inlet and inland from Franklin River.

In 1925, gas car service was extended to Youbou from Victoria, but by 1931, road travel had cut into the revenues sufficiently to prompt the Canadian National to abandon its "galloping goose" after only nine years of operation. During the 1930's, the CNR cut its freight service past Youbou and leased the trackage to Kissinger to Industrial Timber Mills Limited, which operated a large logging railroad in the Cowichan Valley and owned the major sawmill at Youbou.

With the completion of the Tidewater subdivision in 1925 and a new barge slip at Point Ellice, Victoria in 1927, freight passing through the terminal at Patricia Bay dwindled. By the mid-1930's, the Sidney mill had closed and local traffic had declined to a point where there was little justification for keeping the tracks open. After a severe winter which damaged the barge slip at Patricia Bay, the decision was reached to abandon the Patricia Bay line north of Lake Hill three miles from Victoria. In 1935, Ten-Wheeler No. 1438 took a work train out to begin the dismantling operations. Many sections of the original right-of-way still exist, and it is possible with a little effort to walk along most of the once busy route to Sidney.

The winter of 1937 produced one of the few fatal accidents ever to occur on the Cowichan subdivision. Engineer Robert "Frosty" Winters was running a light train with 2-8-0 No. 2112 westbound from Victoria, clearing the line after the Christmas shut-down. As the locomotive started onto the 130-foot trestle over Wolf Creek, the footings, eroded by debris washed down the creek, gave way. The ten miles per hour speed of the locomotive was insufficient to carry it across the bridge. The engine heeled over onto its side at a 45-degree angle and crashed into the enbankment. Caught between the engine and the tender, engineer Winters was scalded by escaping steam. The fireman, Stanley Foreman jumped from the cab as the locomotive crashed through the bridge and was carried downstream. He made his way back to the train and tried to free the engineer, but

Moguls like No. 424 were used in light service on all parts of the CN's Vancouver Island operations. This locomotive was photographed at Ogden Point. — GERALD M. BEST COLLECTION

Stocky oil-burning 4-6-0 No. 1158 saw service on Vancouver Island and was finally preserved in Saskatoon, Saskatchewan. — GERALD M. BEST COLLECTION

CN No. 2112 was typical of numerous 2-8-0's that operated for many years on the Cowichan and Tidewater subdivisions. — STAN F. STYLES

Canadian National Railways' No. 2141, perhaps the best known of all the CN's Vancouver Island locomotives, steams across Holt Creek trestle in a spectacular display of steam and smoke. It is working eastbound from Youbou to Cowichan Bay on January 28, 1958 in the last year of steam operations. The 2141 eventually went to Kamloops for display; an ambitious restoration program began in the 1990's.—DAVE WILKIE

passed out in the attempt. The other crew members cut into the telephone lines paralleling the tracks and called for assistance. A relief train was rushed from Victoria to the scene of the accident. The crew had meanwhile freed the engineer, who was rushed to the hospital in Victoria, where he died that night. Engineer Winters' locomotive survived for many years on the roster of the Cowichan subdivision.

At Cowichan Bay, No. 2149 switches carloads of lumber beside the freighter *British Monarch.* — Dave Wilkie

The locomotives used on Canadian National's Vancouver Island operations have always been small. They were typical examples of types used on branch lines all across Canada, where rails were light and traffic moderate. Until the mid-1920's, service was supplied by a number of light 2-6-0 type Moguls and somewhat heavier Ten-Wheelers. These machines handled most of the switching as well as all of the main line freight trains. Originally all of the locomotives were coal-fired, but it became the practice of both the Canadian National and the Esquimalt and Nanaimo Railway to use only oil-fired engines on Vancouver Island in order to reduce fire danger along the forested lines and to improve the economy of the operations. By the late 1920's, main line trains on the Cowichan subdivision were taken over by heavier, more powerful Class M 2-8-0s, originally built for the Canadian Northern by Montreal Locomotive Works and the Canadian Locomotive Company. These machines handled the bulk of all freight traffic on the Canadian National's Vancouver Island operations until the end of steam railroading.

Yard duties at Port Ellice were usually handled by either a 2-6-0 or an 0-6-0 type switcher like No. 7252 shown in this 1953 photograph. — Stan F. Styles

Locomotives on the CN's Vancouver Island branches were frequently exchanged with others operating out of Port Mann on the mainland. Generally, the lifespan of CNR locomotives on Vancouver Island was quite short; they would be sent to the Island for a few years prior to a major overhaul or retirement. As a result, the Cowichan and Patricia Bay subdivisions built up quite an impressive roster of locomotives over the years.

The last steam locomotives to arrive on the Island for sustained service on the Cowichan subdivision were two relatively modern Class M3 Consolidations, Nos. 2141 and 2149. Both were assigned to freight service out of Victoria in the mid-1950's. They operated very well for the few short years before the first diesels took over on the main line. However, by the fall of 1958, steam railroading had come to an end on the Cowichan subdivision. The economy of the diesel could not

Men like Lou Kellie kept aging CNR steam locomotives in operation until the late 1950's. Here engineer Kellie oils No. 2149. — Provincial Archives

Tyup on the Tidewater subdivision was a busy fuel and water stop during the years of steam operation. — Stan F. Styles

be denied. The aging steam locomotives were spending too much time in the shops and their fuel consumption was too high.

The No. 2141 made her last run from Cowichan Bay to Victoria on July 4, 1958, and was stored outside the Point Ellice engine house pending an uncertain future. The No. 2149 then became the last operating steam locomotive on the Cowichan subdivision, eventually being transferred in late 1958 to the CN's locomotive pool in Edmonton, Alberta. Another Vancouver Island veteran, No. 1158, a 4-6-0, was retired for preservation at Saskatoon, Saskatchewan where it is now on display. The No. 2141 lingered longer, rusting outside the Point Ellice shops at Victoria. Finally, in March 1961, it was shipped over to the mainland for refurbishing in preparation for preservation in Kamloops in the interior of British Columbia. By the end of the following year, all of the facilities on

Port Ellice in Victoria was home base for the Canadian National on Vancouver Island. In this 1949 winter scene, No. 2103 backs from the shops toward the water tower. (RIGHT) Two other 2-8-0's, Nos. 2100 and 2104, rest outside the five-stall engine house where the locomotives were serviced. — Both Elwood White

the Cowichan subdivision for servicing steam locomotives, including the shops, engine house, and water towers had been torn down.

The first diesels to be tried out by the CNR on Vancouver Island were three 1,000 h.p. road switchers built by the Montreal Locomotive Works. However, after several months of operation, they were replaced by similar General Motors units. These locomotives were really elongated yard diesels and are unique to the CNR. They were rated in 1,200 h.p. and were equipped with three-axle trucks to distribute the locomotive's weight in order to minimize damage to the roadbed. The new diesels proved very satisfactory on the light rail and moderate grades encountered on Vancouver Island. Yard work was handled by four light General Electric yard diesels, CN's Nos. 3, 4, 5, and 74. The last three alternated between Ogden Point where the CN operated a small terminal railway, and Point Ellice in Victoria. The No. 3 was assigned to switching operations at the Cowichan Bay docks.

Steam on the Cowichan subdivision was in its last days when 2-8-0 No. 2149, the last active steam locomotive on the line, led CN diesel road-switcher No. 1727 over the Colquitz Creek trestle on September 5, 1958. — Dave Wilkie

Nearing Youbou, a Canadian National GMD-1 road-switcher rumbles along over weed-covered trackage skirting the shore of Cowichan Lake. The engineer of the train is Bill Mellon, a veteran of many years' service on CN lines throughout B. C. — ROBERT D. TURNER

During the late 1950's and early 1960's yard work around Victoria was performed by these General Electric diesels. In the background is the car ferry *Canora*. — VICTORIA PRESS COLLECTION (LEFT) Trailing only one flatcar and a wooden caboose, No. 1030 eases across the long trestle over the Koksilah River. — ROBERT D. TURNER

At Cowichan Bay a CN road-switcher unloads a railway car barge. All traffic to and from Cowichan Lake and Youbou passes through this facility. — Robert D. Turner

Bringing up the rear of a short westbound freight is a typical CN wooden caboose. The two-car train is rolling through Milnes Landing toward Sooke Lake and Deerholme.—Robert D. Turner

Rail traffic between Victoria and Cowichan Lake declined throughout the late 1950's and early 1960's, as the timber resources of the area became depleted and as trucks became more competitive for the comparatively short hauls on the Island. By September 1965, through freight traffic on the main line was dropped, when two trestles west of Victoria failed to meet safety standards It had been the intention of the Canadian National Railways to repair the structures, work having begun in 1960 to replace the timber trestle over the Colquitz River with a concrete and steel structure. However, with the concrete abutments constructed and the steel spans ready for installation, the decision was reversed. Soon after, all but three locomotives were withdrawn from service on Vancouver Island. One road switcher was retained to work the yard shift at Point Ellice and to maintain freight service to a number of industries along a short section of line north of the yards. A second road switcher was used to haul lumber produced by the large B.C. Forest Products mill at Youbou to Cowichan Bay. Occasional freight runs also operated from Deerholme as far south as Colwood. At Ogden Point a yard diesel served the grain elevator and other port facilities.

The last vestige of the old days of steam power on the Cowichan subdivision came to an end in 1968 when the *Canora* was retired after 49 years in the Canadian National's coast service. Over the years the old ship won the affection of many who saw her off the Victoria waterfront or from other points along her frequent runs from the transfer dock on the Fraser River to Victoria and Cowichan Bay. Sold for scrap, she was cut up some years later.

Logging railroads had but one purpose — to haul logs from the forests to the mills on the coast. Here, in a scene that might have been photographed at a dozen locations on Vancouver Island, International Timber Company's Shay No. 4 heads a long train of prime logs towards Campbell River in 1928. — LEONARD FRANK PHOTOS

5

LOGGING RAILROADS

WHEN Europeans first came to the coast of British Columbia late in the eighteenth century, they found the steep mountain slopes and glacier scoured valley bottoms covered by a dense growth of mature evergreen forests. These vast stands of timber were a hindrance to the early settlers attempting to establish farms and villages, but to the loggers who began to operate in the area in the late 1800's, the trees presented all the possibilities of an untapped gold mine. The stands seemed endless and inexhaustible.

Transporting the mature timber on land was in those days almost an impossibility. Yet, the rugged and indented coast line made it possible for lumbermen to harvest the forests with little difficulty. Trees on the slopes above the shore line could be cut and felled directly into the water, where they could be managed with much greater ease. As the years passed, this readily available timber was exhausted, and the loggers were forced to move inland. Here, other logging methods had to be used. Often only the smaller logs, which could be handled by teams of bulls or horses were harvested. "Corduroy roads," little more than trails through the woods paved with small logs laid crosswise on the surface, were built to facilitate the dragging of logs to the nearest waterway. Often it was necessary to apply copious quantities of grease to the logs in order to start the loads moving and then to sand the roads further down as the logs gathered momentum. These procedures were hazardous and inefficient. The growing demand for forest products placed pressures on the loggers to increase their output, but the limits of the early transportation systems had been reached.

Shortly before the turn of the century, the search for a more efficient and productive method of moving large timber from the woods led loggers to the steam locomotive. When the first locomotives were placed in service in the woods of Vancouver Island, timbermen merely adapted the newly acquired machines to their existing skid road systems. Light steel or peeled poles were laid over the old grades, which were improved somewhat to allow for the limited climbing ability of the locomotives. The logs were still "dogged" together, with steel cable, like links in a chain, and dragged downgrade to the shore. The ritual of alternately greasing and sanding the logs and skid roads continued. While the quantity of timber which could be moved increased significantly with the use of locomotives, this method of transport left a great deal to be desired. The dangers of the logs "running away" downgrade or jackknifing at

Before the advent of logging railroads on the coast, teams of bulls or horses were used to drag the logs over corduroy skid roads to the nearest waterway. (RIGHT) Where the terrain permitted, log chutes and flumes simplified the process of getting the timber out of the woods. — BOTH PROVINCIAL ARCHIVES

the bottom of a slope were still present.

In some of the more progressive logging operations, standard railway flatcars were used to haul logs. These were sturdy and had the advantage of being compatable with the equipment used on the main line railroads, should interchange be desirable. Where more flexibility was required, disconnecting trucks were used. These were really little more than heavy freight car trucks, with a coupler or link and pin housing mounted at each end. Across the center bolster, a log bunk was placed, and the logs were spanned across a pair of trucks. With this arrangement, it was possible to accommodate even the longest logs, and hence the loggers were given much more flexibility in the selection of timber. One major drawback of the disconnecting truck was the braking system. Each truck had to be braked by hand, and the crews were forced either to run along beside the trains, applying the brakes as necessary or to ride the loads and attempt to work the brakes from the moving train. Many a brakeman lost an arm or a leg in this risky operation; others never lived to tell of their experiences.

Eventually the awkward disconnecting trucks all but disappeared from the logging railroads. They were replaced by the so-called "skeleton log buggy." Its construction was simple; two standard freight car trucks were separated by three 10x10-inch timbers bolted together or by a pole of comparable dimensions. On either end of the car a log bunk was placed over the center of the trucks. With this type of car, it was possible to apply modern air braking systems to the log trains, and the chance of accidents was greatly reduced.

The skeleton log cars and disconnecting trucks are only two examples of the specialized equipment developed for the logging railroads. The

The first logging railroads on Vancouver Island were primitive operations. Frequently locomotives were used to drag logs between the rails, as in this view of an early Victoria Lumber Company rail line near Chemainus shortly after 1900. — PROVINCIAL ARCHIVES

In their search for more powerful locomotives, the loggers sometimes acquired aging machines from the main line railroads. Victoria Lumber Company's No. 21, shown here at the Chemainus booming grounds, was originally No. 248 on the Pennsylvania Railroad. Note the cordwood piled high in the tender and the use of disconnecting log trucks in this 1900 vintage scene. — PROVINCIAL ARCHIVES

Three types of logging cars were used in the woods of Vancouver Island over the years: flat cars; skeleton cars; and detached or disconnecting trucks. Before the application of air brakes the detached trucks were popular. These consisted of a four-wheel railroad truck carrying bunks. Logs laid across the two trucks made up a car to be coupled to a train. The weight of the logs spanned between the trucks was usually sufficient to keep the train together. The skeleton car consisted of two four-wheel trucks connected by a large center beam; there was no floor on the car. The skeleton car proved highly flexible and durable for use on Vancouver Island. These cars were also safer to operate because air brakes could be used on the car and the train fully connected. On Vancouver Island a skeleton car was less likely to lose its load on the steep twisting grades that characterized many logging lines. Flat cars, while strong and durable, could accumulate large quantities of bark and debris on their decks and were much heavier than a skeleton car of similar capacity.—BOTH GOLDEN WEST COLLECTION

DETACHED or DISCONNECTING TRUCK

SKELETON CAR

The steam donkey engine used in yarding and loading the logs was as much a part of the logging operations as were the locomotives. In this 1940 scene, a long train of skeleton cars is being pulled past the loader on the Port Renfrew railroad of the Hemmingsen-Cameron Company. — BRITISH COLUMBIA FOREST SERVICE (BELOW) In 1912, the Weist Logging Company Ltd. opened its logging railroad near Port Alberni. In this scene, the crew of brakemen poses on top of the impressive loads as the railway's Shay locomotive eases the six sets of disconnecting trucks across a hastily constructed bridge. This 42-ton Shay became Alberni Pacific No. 2 in 1918 and would survive until the 1950s to be preserved by MacMillan & Bloedel in Port Alberni. In 1984, after an enormous effort by many individuals, *2-Spot* was returned to operation and ran for 10 years along the Alberni water-front on excursions. — LEONARD FRANK PHOTOS

To many people, the Shay locomotive and the logging railroad are inseparable. Here in an early Leonard Frank photo, Shay No. 2 of the Cathels and Sorenson Company is posed with five carloads of prime timber near the company camp at Port Renfrew. The photograph clearly shows the driving system of the Shay and provides a glimpse of the dense west coast rain forest in the background. — VANCOUVER PUBLIC LIBRARY

locomotives used were as unusual and individualistic as the loggers themselves. Few machines were standardized in any way. Many were successively rebuilt by four or five different owners to such an extent that the original machine became almost unrecognizable. The logging locomotive was of necessity extremely versatile and flexible. It had to be able to operate in either direction with equal ease, as few operators could afford the luxury of turning facilities at the ends of their countless branch lines. It had to be tough and rugged to survive pulling the heavy timber over the tortuous grades of some of the crudest track ever laid in North America.

To meet the specialized needs of the loggers, a number of distinctive types of locomotives were developed. Some were merely modified versions of machines already in use on shortline railroads throughout Canada, the United States, and Mexico, while others were designed and built especially for the steep grades and heavy loads of logging railroads. This latter type was known as the geared locomotive. The most successful geared engine was first developed by a Michigan logger, Ephraim Shay. He designed a locomotive in which a standard engine boiler was mounted over a frame and supported not by the usual large driving wheels but by four-wheel trucks. The locomotive's cylinders were mounted vertically on the right hand side of the boiler, which was offset to the left to counterbalance the added weight. The axles on the trucks were connected to the cylinder and crank shaft assembly by a series of universal joints, gears, and drive shafts. This arrangement gave the machine tremendous flexibility in negotiating sharply curved twisting tracks and, in effect, sufficiently geared down the locomotive to enable it to pull substantial loads even on steep grades. The Shay, as the locomotive was called, could not compete with the conventional rod locomotive for speed, but on any steep grade it could leave an ordinary engine stalled, unable to keep its footing. The Shay locomotive was manufactured by the Lima Locomotive Works in Lima, Ohio, and while the basic design remained the same, continual improvements were made and new features added.

The Climax locomotive was the most successful competitor of the Shay. Shawnigan Lake Lumber Company's diminutive No. 2 was typical of the lighter Climax geared engines. Note the light rail and quickly sawn ties. The bridge is constructed from logs up to two feet in diameter stacked up to meet the required grade. — PROVINCIAL ARCHIVES

The Pacific Coast Shay was the culmination of years of steady improvement in the design of this versatile type of locomotive. Among its most noticeable features are the cast steel trucks, piston valves and heavy steel girder frame. MacMillan and Bloedel's No. 19, shown here at Camp B on the Franklin River operation in 1956, was typical of the design. The machine was Lima No. 3352, and was built in 1938. It was the third-from-the-last Shay ever constructed. — Albert Farrow

The most advanced version of the Shay to operate in the West was the "Pacific Coast" Shay, first shown by Lima at the Pacific Logging Congress in November 1927. It became one of the only types of logging locomotives which could be called standardized. It incorporated all the refinements the Lima Locomotive Works had developed — cast steel trucks, piston valves, a girder frame, and many other internal and external features that made the machine entirely satisfactory. In all, 24 Pacific Coast Shays were built for the west coast loggers. Of these, 17 were used on Vancouver Island. Bloedel, Stewart and Welch Limited, one of the largest operators on the Island, used five of these machines on its Menzies Bay and Franklin River railroads. In 1951, following the series of mergers in which MacMillan and Bloedel Limited was formed, a total of seven Pacific Coast Shays were incorporated onto the roster of that company. This was the largest number owned by any single operator anywhere. A number of other geared locomotives were designed and built to challenge the popularity of the Shay, but none could change the affinity the loggers had developed for this locomotive type.

Another type of geared locomotive which came to be used on the west coast was the Climax. Like the Shay, it made use of a gearing system to power each axle of the supporting trucks. The chief difference was in the arrangement of the gears and cylinders. Whereas most Shays had three cylinders mounted on the right side of the boiler, the Climax had only two, mounted on opposite sides of the boiler. The cylinders were inclined at an angle, with their rods connected to a gearing system carrying the power along a central shaft under the boiler. Climaxes were successful and popular machines, but some considered them hard riding as they tended to buck on rough track. A few of the earlier machines developed a noticeable sway-backed appearance after a few years of operation which made them look much older than they really were.

British Columbia Forest Products' No. 8 (originally Malahat Logging No. 4) was the largest and most modern Heisler to operate on Vancouver Island. Heislers of this type, known as West Coast Specials, were designed to compete with Lima's Pacific Coast Shays. The scene was photographed along the south side of the San Juan River Valley east of Port Renfrew in 1953. Note the cut-over hillsides and the sprinkler system used to protect the trestle from fire. — CAM'S PHOTO SERVICE

In contrast to No. 8, on the opposite page, this Heisler was showing the effects of hard service when photographed in the early 1930s. The 50-ton machine was built in May 1919 for the Capilano Timber Company of North Vancouver as their No. 3. It later operated for the Sisters Creek Logging Company and was eventually leased to Thomsen and Clark at Horne Lake on Vancouver Island. The machine was scrapped in 1938. —ALBERT H. PAULL

The other machine completing the trio of popular geared locomotives was the Heisler. Unlike the Shay and the Climax, it was never used extensively on Vancouver Island. Less than a dozen were employed by loggers on the Island. In the Heisler, use was made of a slightly different system of transferring power from the locomotive's cylinders to the wheels. The cylinders were mounted in a 'V' position around the boiler. Power was transmitted through a central shaft connecting with only one axle of each truck. A driving rod was connected to each wheel, making the locomotive almost a hybrid, with mechanical features of both geared and rod engines.

One other type of geared engine, built by the Willamette Iron Works of Portland, Oregon, was used successfully in west coast logging. Known officially as the Willamette, and popularly as the Willamette Shay, it was built after some of the patents for the Shay locomotive expired in the 1920's and was basically a refined version of the Lima Shay. Only one of these locomotives was ever used on Vancouver Island.

No. 3 of Lake Logging Company at Cowichan Lake was the only Willamette locomotive to operate on Vancouver Island. In this 1937 scene, the engine is working a long train of logs to the dump. As Western Forest Industries No. 3, the 70-ton machine was scrapped in July 1956. — BRITISH COLUMBIA FOREST SERVICE

The McDonald Murphy Logging Company, the original owner of the Willamette locomotive illustrated in the center photograph, used this homemade speeder at its Cowichan Lake operation. The speeder is also shown in the center photo.—CEDRIC MYERS—JOHN HOFFMEISTER COLLECTION

B. C. Mills Timber and Trading Company of Rock Bay, on the northeast coast of Vancouver Island, had a sizeable roster of tank locomotives on its early operation. Here, No. 7 and a train of disconnecting log trucks wait while a load is assembled for the last car. — LEONARD FRANK PHOTOS

The conventional rod locomotives also underwent a number of modifications to make them more suited for use in the woods. Nearly all were fitted with small driving wheels to give them extra tractive power. This had the added advantage of shortening the wheel base, making it easier for the machines to negotiate sharp curves. Often the center driving wheels were flangeless, further increasing the adaptability to curved track. Nearly all logging locomotives were equipped with lead and trailing wheels, both to help support the weight of the locomotive and to aid the machine in picking its way over the roughly laid track. Often, companies would operate rod engines in conjunction with geared locomotives. Shays, Climaxes, and Heislers would be used to bring loaded cars down over the steep grades to the valley bottoms, where the faster rod engines would take over to haul them to the booming grounds.

Comox and Campbell Lake Tramway Company, the predecessor of Comox Logging and Railway Company, operated this classic wood-burning 2-6-2. The locomotive was built by Baldwin in 1909. — LEONARD FRANK PHOTOS

Tank engines, which carried water in a tank placed over or on each side of the boiler instead of in a tender, were a popular type of locomotive in the woods. They operated equally well in both directions and had the advantage of carrying nearly all their weight directly over the driving wheels. They varied in size from small 15 or 20-ton machines with four or six drivers to large articulated engines weighing over 150 tons and having a 2-6-6-2 wheel arrangement. Tank engines found their way into the roster of nearly every major logging railroad on Vancouver Island. In fact, the last regularly operating rod engine is a 2-8-2T built by the Baldwin Locomotive Works.

Tank locomotives like this Baldwin 2-8-2 were used extensively in the logging industry. No. 3 ended her career with the Alberni Pacific Lumber Company which scrapped the engine for parts. Her sister, the No. 2, ultimately became MacMillan Bloedel No. 1055, which still survives. — H. L. BROADBELT COLLECTION

LOGGING CAMPS

The isolated backwoods logging camp was once common on Vancouver Island. In the first half of the 20th-century, nearly every operation of any size featured one or more semi-portable communities like those pictured on these pages. Typically, a camp included bunkhouses, a kitchen and mess hall, offices, machine shops and sometimes married quarters and a school. Many of the buildings or camp cars were designed as individual units so they they could be moved from place to place. Conditions in the camps varied tremendously, generally improving as the years progressed. Some were spotless communities but others were dirty shack towns. On the left is a view of Victoria Lumber Company's Camp 5 west of Ladysmith as it appeared in 1907. The Chinese cook is about to beat the triangle calling the loggers to the mess hall as a locomotive bears down on the scene.—Provincial Archives (BELOW) B.C. Mills Timber and Trading Company's camp near Rock Bay represented a more modern, clean and permanent facility. In this 1920 scene, the loggers pose with two of the line's tank locomotives. The buildings on the left are bunkhouses while the large unpainted structure in the background at right is the locomotive shop.—LEONARD FRANK PHOTOS

It is late in the afternoon and International Timber Company's Shay No. 2 has just returned from the woods with a crew car bringing the loggers back to camp. Frequently the logging companies used old passenger coaches or rebuilt boxcars to carry the crews to and from the spurs where timber cutting was in progress. Specially built speeders were also common, particularly in the years following the Second World War. Notice that many of the camp buildings are mounted on railroad trucks for easy movement when the logging operations became too far removed from the campsite. This scene was recorded in the vicinity of Campbell River on June 5, 1926.—A. A. PAULL—VANCOUVER PUBLIC LIBRARY

Shawnigan Lake Lumber Company operated this 1902 vintage Class A Climax. Originally the locomotive was equipped with double flanged wheels for running on poles as running rails. In later years steel rails were substituted and standard railroad wheels applied as the company extended further and further into the woods.— PROVINCIAL ARCHIVES

The function and character of logging railroads changed dramatically over the years in response to technological improvements and economic conditions. While some large operations, such as Comox Logging and Railway Company and Bloedel, Stewart and Welch Limited began large scale logging early in their histories, the majority of the first logging railroads were small, contrasting significantly with the complex systems which developed in later years. Usually, one or two individuals would acquire the rights to a block of timber and would sell their logs to the large mill operations along the coast. Business was full of risks; sudden price fluctuations could make or break the small operator. Still, if timber prices held, there was a good chance of clearing a substantial profit. The philosophy of the operators was "cut and get out." No thought was given to such concepts as sustained yield and reforestation. Such operators usually owned only one or two locomotives and six to ten log cars. Since capital was always scarce, seldom were more than two miles of track in use at one time. As the timber was cut, the rails were ripped up and relaid again and again into uncut forests.

During the period from 1900 to 1915, exports of lumber from British Columbia fell each year as competition from American producers increased. The province's share of world lumber sales had declined from 30 percent to a meagre five percent, while the American share rose 37 percent during the same period. In an attempt to regain foreign markets, British Columbia lumber producers began to ship their products to Salina Cruz, Mexico, for rail transport to the Gulf of Mexico. From there the shipments were taken to England by steamer. Changes in tariff regulations and the opening of the Panama Canal in 1914 greatly improved the competitive position of the province, and the forest industry in British Columbia began a rapid expansion.

Climax No. 2 of the Shawnigan Lake Lumber Co. looked mighty small indeed when compared with some of the giant logs it was expected to move to the log dump. This 23-ton machine, built in 1910, came to the Shawnigan Lake line brand new. — PROVINCIAL ARCHIVES

As demands for forest products grew during World War I and the early 1920's, the number of small logging railroads on Vancouver Island increased substantially. All along the coast, and around the major lakes, small quickly constructed railroads were laid into the timber stands. Luxuries such as well graded right-of-ways and ballast were unheard of on these lines. Railroads built in this hurried fashion cost as little as $5,000 per mile. The operators used every means at hand to reduce the costs still further. By present standards some of their techniques were very wasteful. Bridges were frequently built using newly felled trees stacked and piled by the hundreds to maintain the required grade. It was simply cheaper and more expedient to use the materials at hand rather than importing cut timber or pilings for trestle

The Royston Lumber Company which operated near Courtenay during the 1920's and 1930's was typical of the smaller operations on Vancouver Island. The small locomotive is a 2-4-2T, their No. 2. — JOHN LOCKNER

VANCOUVER ISLAND LOGGING RAILROADS - 1925

Company	Operating	MILES: TRACK	LOCOMOTIVES	FLAT CARS	LOG CARS	DISCONNECTING TRUCKS	OTHER EQUIPMENT
Alberni Pacific Lumber Co. Ltd.	Alberni District	7.00	2	–	44	–	5
Bainbridge Logging Co. Ltd.	Bainbridge	4.50	1	–	–	20	1
Beaver Cove Lumber & Pulp Co. Ltd.	Beaver Cove	1.75	1	–	8	–	4
F. Beban Lumber Company	Extension	2.00	1	–	6	–	1
Bloedel Stewart & Welch Ltd. (also operated on mainland B. C.)	Union Bay	17.50	2	3	50	2	3
B. & K. Logging Co. Ltd.	Elk Bay	4.50	1	–	9	–	3
B. C. Mills Timber & Trading Co. Ltd.	Rock Bay	22.00	4	2	–	121	10
Cameron Lumber Co. Ltd.	Mile 54, CNR	2.25	1	(used CN equip.)			
Canadian Robert Dollar Co. Ltd.	Deep Bay	4.25	1	–	15	–	2
Cathels & Sorensen	Port Renfrew	9.50	2	1	21	8	5
Channel Logging Co. Ltd.	Cowichan	2.00	1	(used CN equip.)			
Comox Logging & Railway Co. Ltd.	Comox District	55.00	7	200	–	–	28
Dawson Taylor Logging Co.	Courtenay	1.75	1	–	–	2	–
Deep Bay Logging Co. Ltd.	Fanny Bay	1.25	–	–	–	–	–
Eastern Lumber Co. (narrow gauge)	Ladysmith	2.50	1	2	–	–	–
Gwilt Lumber Co. Ltd.	Puntledge	2.00	1	–	1	–	–
Hillcrest Lumber Co.	Sahtlam	1.00	1	–	3	–	–
International Timber Company Ltd.	Campbell River	35.00	4	2	65	–	38
Island Logging Co. Ltd.	Charter Siding	11.00	2	(used E&N equip.)			
James Logging Co. Ltd.	Cowichan Lake Dist.	5.00	1	1	25	–	3
Lake Lumber Co. Ltd.	Qualicum Beach	2.50	1	–	3	–	–
Lamb Lumber Co. Ltd.	Menzies Bay	12.50	2	1	45	8	3
Mayo Lumber Co.	Mayo Siding	3.00	3	–	16	–	–
Merrill & Ring Lumber Co. Ltd.	Duncan Bay	6.00	3	–	36	–	8
MacDonald-Murphy Co. Ltd.	Cowichan Lake	4.00	1	–	2	–	2
New Ladysmith Lumber Co. Ltd.	East Wellington	12.00	2	2	5	6	2
Royston Lumber Co. Ltd.	Cumberland	2.25	1	–	4	–	–
Scottish Logging Co. Ltd.	Mile 65, CNR	1.50	1	(used CN equip.)			
Shawnigan Lake Lumber Co. Ltd.	Shawnigan Lake	4.00	2	–	12	8	–
Sing Chong Logging Railway	Fanny Bay	2.00	1	–	2	–	–
Superior Lumber Co.	Nanoose Bay	2.25	1	–	–	2	–
Thomsen & Clark Timber Co. Ltd.	Deep Bay	17.50	2	7	–	40	9
Timberland Development Co. Ltd.	Ladysmith	18.00	2	9	17	8	10
Victoria Lumber & Manufacturing Co. Ltd.	Chemainus	13.50	3	2	21	38	8
	Haslam Creek	10.00	1	–	10	54	18
Under construction:	Cowichan Lake	8.25	1	–	–	–	6
J. C. Wilson Lumber Co.	Qualicum Beach	3.50	1	–	–	5	1
Wood & English Ltd.	Englewood	42.50	4	8	89	15	17

construction. Ties too were often made on the site of construction. Small trees were cut to approximately the right length and were sawn along one side to give a flat spiking surface. The use of tie plates and creosote for the ties was not even considered.

These free wheeling days did not go on indefinitely. Gradually the timber was cut further inland and the loggers were forced to either expand their railroads or go out of business. Additionally, new logging trucks were being developed which could compete favorably with the railroads in short haul operations. It was estimated that for distances under ten miles both trucks and railroads could haul 1,000 board-feet of timber for about $2.75. The advantage inherent in trucks was that they were able to use rough roads which cost from $2,000 to $3,000 per mile less than a railroad to construct. Under these circumstances, it is not surprising that many of the small operators sold their railroad equipment and bought trucks.

The logging railroad on Vancouver Island had entered the second phase of its development. Railroads could no longer be operated on a small scale. Increasing costs of equipment and the longer hauls involved necessitated the construction of

Clear cut logging has a devastating effect on the landscape. In the early days when reforestation was unheard of or ignored, and before fire control became effective, the forests suffered badly. Few were concerned about forest management when the resources seemed limitless. The scene above shows the Menzies Bay operations of Lamb Lumber Company in 1926. The locomotives are Climax No. 2 and Shay No. 1. (BELOW) With at least 24 carloads of logs behind the water car, which was carried in case of fire, International Timber Company No. 4 eases into camp near Campbell River in June 1926.
—Both A. A. Paull—Vancouver Public Library

By the 1930's railroad logging had become big business on Vancouver Island, requiring a large investment in structures and equipment. Malahat Logging's trestle over Bear Creek was the largest wooden bridge on Vancouver Island. The illustration on the left shows the bridge as it appeared in 1953, when British Columbia Forest Products Limited was operating the line. — CAM'S PHOTO SERVICE

more permanent facilities and right-of-ways. Economic conditions also hastened the formation of larger companies; during the depression years only the bigger producers could survive.

The larger logging companies had railroad facilities beyond the imagination of the early loggers. Roadbeds were built to much higher standards, and gorges which in earlier years would have been impassable were bridged with spectacular timber and pile trestles. Locomotives were bigger and more variable; a company's roster would often include five or six geared engines in addition to the rod engines employed on the main lines.

The railroad was still a vital part of the actual timber cutting operations. Tracks were laid to the timber and the logs were loaded directly onto the railway cars by steam powered donkey engines. These were rigged with elaborate systems of blocks and cables to large "spar" trees and were employed as mobile winches and yarders to assemble the logs on the cars. The donkey engine evolved into a machine of tremendous proportion known as a tower skidder. This machine incorporated a yarder with steel tower and a loader and was mounted on railway trucks. Many stories are told of the problems encountered moving the monstrous tower skidders, many of which weighed up to 300 tons. Generally two or more locomotives were required to keep the machine in control. It

At Crofton, the Osborn Bay Wharf Company operated one of the last Shays to see service on Vancouver Island. In the view above, the little coal burner is switching lumber flats beside the Liberty ship *Kyma*. The locomotive now operates at the Cowichan Valley Forest Museum near Duncan. — STAN F. STYLES

Loading freshly cut timber directly onto rail cars became less frequent as the timber was removed from the lowlands. The scene above shows a large steam loader at work for British Columbia Forest Products near Nitinat in 1950. (UPPER RIGHT) By the 1950's most rail lines operated to permanent log transfer points serviced by diesel trucks. — BOTH CAM'S PHOTO SERVICE

was necessary to space skeleton cars between the skidder and the locomotives to distribute the weight of the train and prevent damage to the roadbed or bridges. If the skidder was ever derailed the crews could be sure of having a mammoth task ahead of them.

During the late 1930's, increasing numbers of diesel trucks were employed in log hauling. In addition, diesel yarders and loaders began replacing the familiar donkey engines at the logging sites. Although World War II retarded this trend, the gradual switch to diesel operations was inevitable. Other changes in the structure and operation of logging railways were also beginning to take place.

Intensive logging had exhausted most of the stands of timber occupying the valley bottoms and lower hillsides of the Island. Logging railroads were costly and inefficient on the upper slopes of the hills. Modern logging trucks were much more suitable for these conditions, although they could not readily match the efficiency of well established rail lines in hauling logs along the valley bottoms to the coast. Consequently, in several areas the final phase of the evolution of logging railroads, in which they were used in combination with trucks, was ushered in. Diesel trucks hauled newly cut logs from the mountain slopes to a centrally located site, where the loads were transferred to railroad cars. Thus, the railroad became a main line log hauling operation, quite removed from the actual timber cutting process. This new system provided a reprieve for many logging railroads, which otherwise would have been torn up and scrapped.

The last Shay working for the forest industry was Elk Falls Company's No. 1 shown here in 1968 unloading chemical tank cars at the Duncan Bay pulp mill where the locomotive used its pulling power to advantage. In 1974 it was donated to the National Museum of Science and Technology in Ottawa. There, volunteers have fully restored the locomotive to operation. — ROBERT D. TURNER

Hillcrest Lumber Company of Mesachie Lake was the last operator of Climax locomotives, other than in tourist service, in Canada and the United States. As a result its No. 10, shown above, and No. 9, at left, received wide attention. No. 10 was eventually moved to the Mount Rainier Scenic Railroad at Elbe, Washington, and No. 9 to the British Columbia Forest Museum for preservation. No. 9 visited the California State Railroad Museum at Sacramento in 1991. (OPPOSITE PAGE) No. 10 ambles along through wild flowers that have overgrown the tracks near Mesachie Lake.—ALL ROBERT D. TURNER

Ironically, in the late 1940's and early 1950's, when many logging railroads were being closed down, the largest individual logging railroad operations in the history of British Columbia were formed. By a series of purchases and mergers most of the remaining logging railroads were consolidated into the holdings of four companies: British Columbia Forest Products Limited, Canadian Forest Products, Ltd. (Canfor), Canadian Western Lumber Company (later a subsidiary of Crown Zellerbach Canada Limited), and MacMillan Bloedel Limited. Still, much of the equipment was soon disposed of and only a few railroad operations remained in service beyond the mid-1950's. Under special circumstances, however, logging railroads have survived even to the present day. Where they have lasted they have proved to

"Sounding like 60 and going 10" characterized all of the geared locomotives operated by the loggers. Hillcrest's No. 10 was no exception. Here, as it churns along at about 12 miles per hour, its Walschaert valve gear is a blur of motion.—ROBERT D. TURNER

be an effective and economical means of transporting timber. After a series of test runs, Crown Zellerbach's Comox Logging and Canadian Forest Products both switched to diesels and upgraded their equipment, making the railroads competitive with trucking.

After the end of steam-powered log hauling, several steam locomotives were kept in operation at mills as switchers. MacMillan Bloedel's No. 1055 ran at Chemainus for several years after its log hauling days ended in 1969. Another 2-8-2T, No. 1066, was also retained for a few years before both locomotives were preserved. TheElk Falls Company at Duncan Bay, near Campbell River, used its Shay No. 1 at its pulp mill to load and unload cars from railway barges towed in from the mainland. The Shay was used at the mill until it was replaced by Comox Logging's Baldwin diesel which was transferred from log hauling at Ladysmith. Subsequently, the Shay was donated to the National Museum of Science and Technology in Ottawa. The last steam locomotive maintained by the forest industry became Canfor's 113, a large 2-8-2, which the company operated for special occasions and tours after diesels took over the regular log hauling duties.

For many years, until August 1968, Hillcrest Lumber Company at Mesachie Lake employed a Climax, No. 10, for mill switching. Following the closure of the mill, the No. 10 was acquired by private interests. Hillcrest shared trackage to Lake Cowichan with Western Forest Industries which ran a large mill at Honeymoon Bay. After the No. 10 was retired, WFI used a Plymouth diesel on its line until its mill was closed in 1981.

Hillcrest's other Climax, No. 9, was placed on display at the Cowichan Valley Forest Museum (later renamed the British Columbia Forest Museum). This museum, founded by lumberman Gerry Wellburn, became one of the major focuses of railway preservation on Vancouver Island and has many exhibits of early logging machinery. Every summer a steam-powered narrow gauge passenger train is run for the benefit of visitors. One of the highlights of the operation is the museum's two-truck Shay No. 1 which worked in its early days for Hillcrest Lumber and later at Osborn Bay Wharf near Crofton.

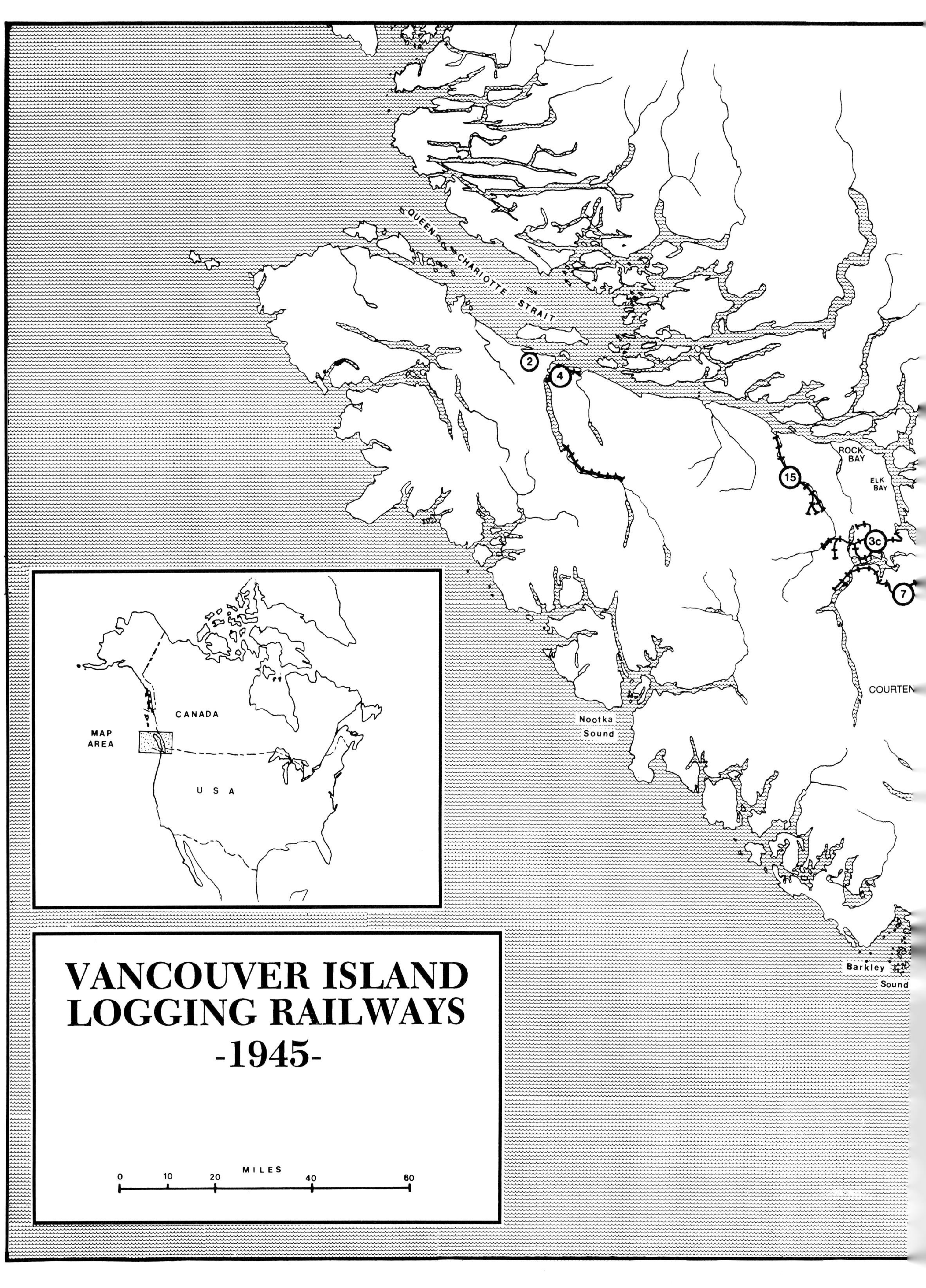

QUEEN CHARLOTTE STRAIT
2
4
15
ROCK BAY
ELK BAY
3c
7
COURTEN
Nootka Sound
Barkley Sound
MAP AREA
CANADA
U S A
VANCOUVER ISLAND LOGGING RAILWAYS
-1945-
MILES
0
10
20
40
60

1	Alberni Pacific Lumber Co., Ltd.	Port Alberni	75.0	Miles
2	B. & D. Logging Company	Hyde Creek	2.0	
3a	Bloedel Stewart & Welch, Ltd.	Great Central	16.0	
3b	Bloedel Stewart & Welch, Ltd.	Franklin River	48.0	
3c	Bloedel Stewart & Welch, Ltd.	Menzies Bay	59.6	
4	Canadian Forest Products, Ltd.	Englewood	28.5	
5a	Comox Logging & Railway Co.	Headquarters	29.0	
5b	Comox Logging & Railway Co.	Nanaimo Lakes	41.1	
6	Deep Bay Logging Co., Ltd.	Fanny Bay	8.1	
7	Elk River Timber Co., Ltd.	Campbell River	72.0	
8	Hemmingsen-Cameron Co., Ltd.	Port Renfrew	19.5	
9	Hillcrest Lumber Co.	Mesachie Lake	17.5	
10a	Industrial Timber Mills, Ltd.	Caycuse	} 36.0	
10b	Industrial Timber Mills, Ltd.	Youbou		
11	Lake Logging Co., Ltd.	Honeymoon Bay	43.8	
12	Malahat Logging Co., Ltd.	Port Renfrew	34.1	
13	Mayo Bros. Timber Co., Ltd.	Paldi	10.0	
14	Pacific Logging Co., Ltd.	Cowichan Lake	5.0	
15	Salmon River Logging Co., Ltd.	Kelsey Bay	37.0	
16a	Victoria Lumber Co., Ltd.	Copper Canyon	39.2	
16b	Victoria Lumber Co., Ltd.	Fanny Bay	16.3	

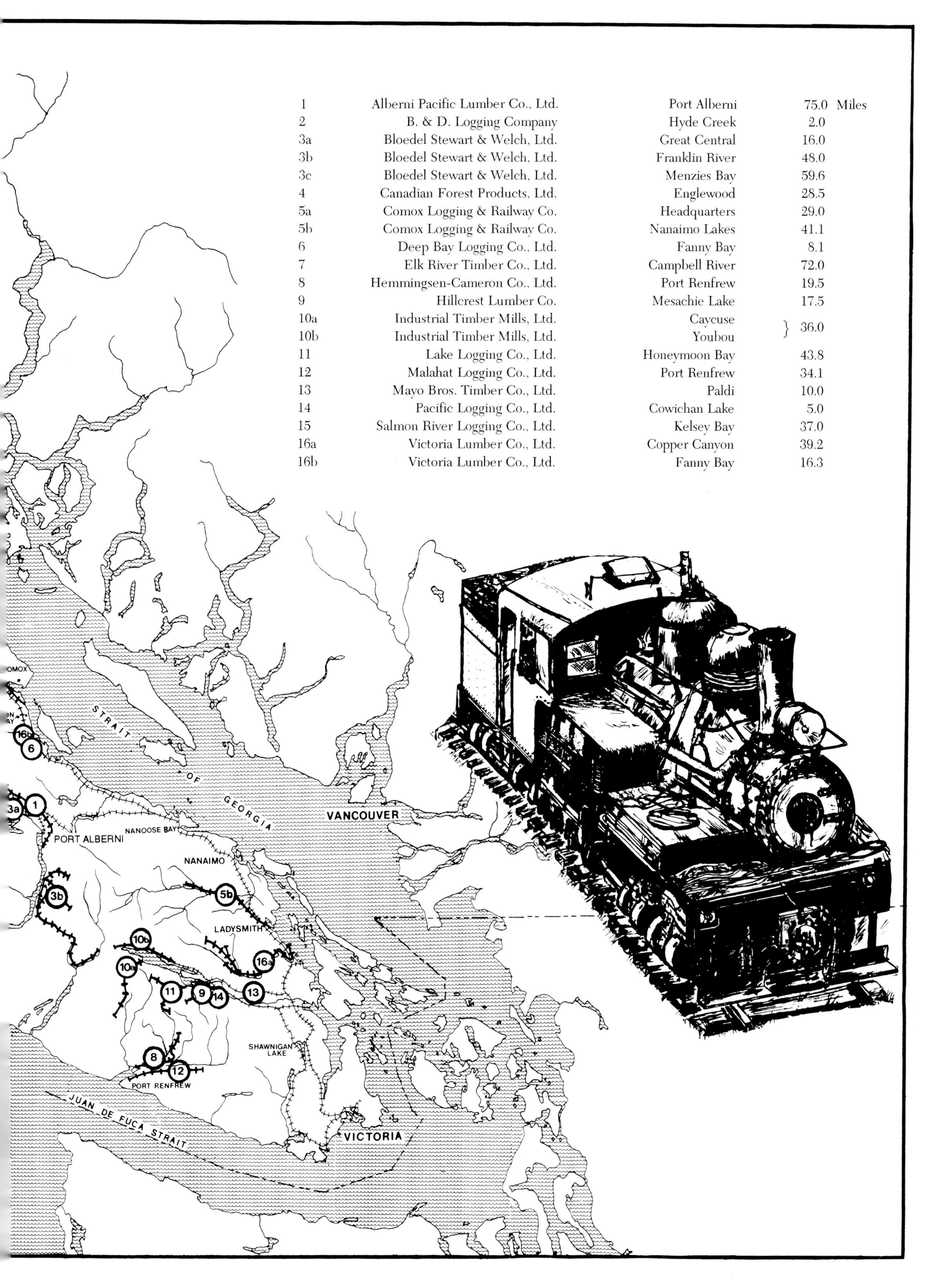

Victoria Lumber and Manufacturing Company's Shay No. 6 was built to carry every ounce of cordwood that could be packed in. Shown here operating out of Chemainus in the 1920's, the machine never strayed far from home. It was scrapped in the early 1950's as MacMillan and Bloedel's first No. 1066. — MacMillan Bloedel Collection

MacMILLAN BLOEDEL LTD.

The corporate history of MacMillan Bloedel Limited is long and complex. It is sufficient to note here that a predecessor of the present company, MacMillan and Bloedel Limited, was formed in 1951 following the merger of Bloedel, Stewart and Welch, Limited and the MacMillan Export Company. Bloedel, Stewart and Welch began logging on the British Columbia coast back in 1911. The rail operations ultimately controlled by the MacMillan Export Company date to the late 1800's. These included the lines of the Victoria Lumber Company (formerly Victoria Lumber and Manufacturing Company) and the Alberni Pacific Lumber Company.

The combined locomotive and equipment rosters of all of the companies incorporated into the holdings of MacMillan Bloedel Limited was impressive. However, many of the inherited lines of the new company were soon abandoned in favor of trucking.

The extensive complex of railroad lines running out of Menzies Bay, operated by Bloedel, Stewart and Welch was phased out in 1953. At this operation, the company employed a number of Shays and Climaxes as well as a heavy 2-8-2 tank engine and a saddle tank Mallet 2-6-6-2 on the main line. One of the Shays at this site was Bloedel, Stewart and Welch's No. 11, the first Pacific Coast Shay built, and remembered as the locomotive displayed at the Pacific Logging Congress in 1927. For a locomotive of such distinguished character, it was fitting that its demise was as spectacular as its introduction to the loggers. In late August 1949, No. 11 was ballasting a section of Branch 61, while a train of log cars was being loaded on the West Main Line. The number of cars to be loaded exceeded the capacity of the track section protected by a derail, so it was planned to bring the Shay up to the loader to hold the train while the last of the logs were loaded. Seeing that the cars would soon overrun the derail, the crew opened it and called the dispatcher to send up the No. 11 early. As one of the last cars was being loaded, the

VL&M's No. 4 (later 1044) was one of those logging engines that went through numerous rebuildings during its career. A photograph of this locomotive as it appeared in later years is shown on page 146. — JACK CASH — MACMILLAN BLOEDEL COLLECTION

Another predecessor of MacMillan Bloedel was Great Central Sawmills Ltd., which operated a large sawmill and railroad. Their No. 2 became BS&W's No. 2 and later No. 15. The locomotive was badly damaged in 1940 and finally scrapped in 1953. — PROVINCIAL ARCHIVES

The Alberni Pacific Lumber Company maintained one of the larger sawmilling and logging railroad operations on Vancouver Island. This scene shows the mill at Port Alberni where a tramp steamer is loading lumber. Also visible is a steam crane and Shay No. 3 to the left of this scene. (RIGHT) A Bloedel Stewart and Welch Shay churns along beside a steep rock face on the Franklin River operation. This logging line utilized sections of the grade built for but not used by the Canadian National. — BOTH VANCOUVER PUBLIC LIBRARY

Bloedel, Stewart & Welch, Ltd.'s No. 4 poses for a classic builder's portrait at the Baldwin Locomotive Works. Note the incorrect spelling of Welch on the tank lettered by Baldwin. This locomotive eventually became MacMillan Bloedel's second 1066 and operated at Chemainus until the end of log hauling. It was subsequently displayed near Squamish and later at Qualicum.—H. L. BROADBELT COLLECTION (BELOW) With 16 cars of fresh logs coupled to its pilot, BS&W's No. 4 posed on the company's Menzies Bay railroad in 1926 soon after its arrival from Baldwin. By this time the spelling of Welch had been corrected.—A. A. PAULL—VANCOUVER PUBLIC LIBRARY

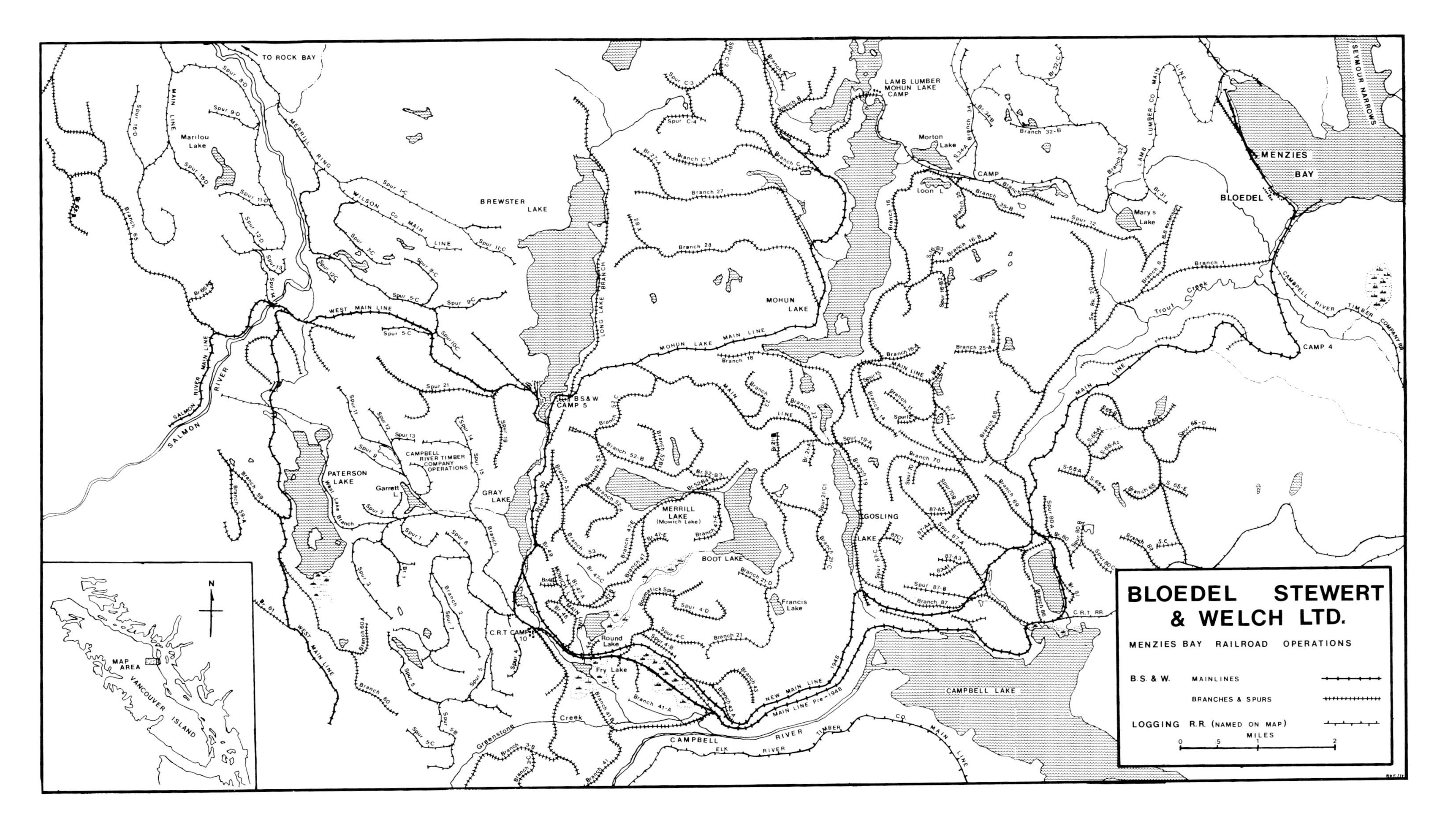
BLOEDEL STEWERT
& WELCH LTD.
MENZIES BAY RAILROAD OPERATIONS
B.S. & W. MAINLINES
BRANCHES & SPURS
LOGGING R.R. (NAMED ON MAP)
MILES
0 .5 1 2
MENZIES BAY
SEYMOUR NARROWS
BLOEDEL
CAMP 4
CAMPBELL RIVER TIMBER COMPANY RR
LAMB LUMBER CO MAIN LINE
LAMB LUMBER MOHUN LAKE CAMP
Morton Lake
Loon L
Mary's Lake
CAMP
MOHUN LAKE
MOHUN LAKE MAIN LINE
BREWSTER LAKE
LONG LAKE BRANCH
BS&W CAMP 5
GOSLING LAKE
MERRILL LAKE
(Mowich Lake)
BOOT LAKE
Francis Lake
Round Lake
Fry Lake
CAMPBELL LAKE
CAMPBELL RIVER
ELK RIVER
TIMBER CO MAIN LINE
NEW MAIN LINE 1948
MAIN LINE Pre-1948
C.R.T. RR
C.R.T CAMP 10
Greenstone Creek
Trout Creek
GRAY LAKE
PATERSON LAKE
Garrett L.
CAMPBELL RIVER TIMBER COMPANY OPERATIONS
West Lake Branch
WEST MAIN LINE
SALMON RIVER
SALMON RIVER MAIN LINE
MERRILL RING WILSON Co MAIN LINE
TO ROCK BAY
Marilou Lake
MAIN LINE
MAP AREA
VANCOUVER ISLAND
N

Victoria Lumber and Manufacturing Company's 2-6-2 No. 4 roars across a heavy log bridge spanning the Chemainus on the Copper Canyon line. — MACMILLAN BLOEDEL COLLECTION (BELOW) The only Mallet articulated locomotive to operate on Vancouver Island was Bloedel, Stewart and Welch's No. 6 shown here at Menzies Bay in 1950. — TED ROBSON

The saddletank 2-6-6-2 ended her days in company with several Pacific Coast Shays at Franklin River. In this view the locomotive is out of service awaiting scrapping. — STAN F. STYLES (BELOW) Pacific Coast Shay No. 1019 takes on fuel at Camp A on the Franklin River operation during July 1955. — ELWOOD WHITE

spotting cable stranded and the loads started rolling downgrade. By this time, the No. 11 was working upgrade towards the loader; all the crew could do was throw the Shay into reverse and hope to couple onto the leading car in motion. The log cars had gained too much momentum however, and one log protruding from the leading car broke a two inch pipe on the No. 11's air reservoir. With the air brakes inoperable, all hope of stopping the runaway was lost. The crew "joined the birds," and the No. 11 clattered down the mile long incline showering parts and pieces in reckless abandon. At the switch to Branch 60, the No. 11 hit a curved trestle and plunged over an embankment.

By the end of the week, operations were more or less back to normal and Climax No. 21 was sent out with the company's 110-ton Bucyrus-Erie Crane to clear up the logs and wrecked skeleton cars. The No. 21 had to wait at the Branch 60 switch for clearance while speeder No. 550 eased a 35-ton "bull car" (a steel decked flat car) down the long incline on the main line. However, the little 4.5-ton speeder could not control the heavy

This homemade caboose was typical of those used by numerous logging railroads along the coast. At the other end of the train, MacMillan Bloedel's No. 1066 eases two dozen log cars in the train down the steep Chemainus switchback. (LEFT) Down at the Chemainus log dump, MacMillan Bloedel No. 1044 shoves a long train of skeleton cars towards the unloader.—BOTH ROBERT D. TURNER

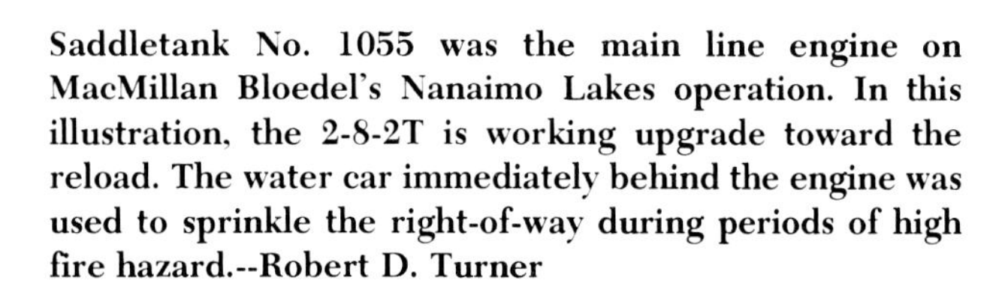

Saddletank No. 1055 was the main line engine on MacMillan Bloedel's Nanaimo Lakes operation. In this illustration, the 2-8-2T is working upgrade toward the reload. The water car immediately behind the engine was used to sprinkle the right-of-way during periods of high fire hazard.--Robert D. Turner

On a frosty winter morning in 1968, No. 1055 coasts downgrade with an impressive train of logs. MacMillan Bloedel trains made their last runs over this line through the Nanaimo River Valley in December 1969. (BELOW) Engineer Bob Strang keeps a careful eye on his locomotive at Chemainus. — BOTH ROBERT D. TURNER

Its work for the day completed, No. 1055 steams up to the water tower at MacMillan Bloedel's Nanaimo Lakes camp. In the distance is 2-6-2 No. 1077, the standby engine on the Nanaimo Lakes line. — ROBERT D. TURNER

car and by the time it came into sight of the No. 21, it was too late. The engine crew succeeded in reversing the train, but the coupling was very rough. The crane swung around and smashed into the smoke box of the unlucky Climax, breaking one of its custom castings, thus effectively ending the career of No. 21.

At the close of the Menzies Bay operation, some of the surviving equipment including the big Mallet, was transferred to Franklin River on the Alberni Inlet, where rail logging was still in progress. This line remained in service until 1958. Plans to move the Mallet once again, never materialized and she was scrapped in 1960.

At the Nanaimo Lakes and Copper Canyon operations of the Victoria Lumber Company, railroading continued under MacMillan and Bloedel ownership. The Copper Canyon line was abandoned in 1955, but the Nanaimo Lakes branch operated throughout the 1950's and 60's, becoming a focal point of interest to rail fans from many parts of North America. This operation was composed of two separate rail lines. One, jointly owned with Comox Logging and Railway Company, ran from the company's railroad camp in the Nanaimo River Valley to the outskirts of Ladysmith. At Ladysmith, Esquimalt and Nanaimo Railway diesels took over and hauled the loaded cars to Chemainus where another MacMillan Bloedel steam locomotive switched the cars down to the log dump. Trucking finally replaced this last steam-powered operation in December 1969 and two of the company's four remaining steam locomotives were retired. One locomotive is operated as a mill switcher at Chemainus.

High above the rushing waters of Bear Creek, British Columbia Forest Products Limited's Heisler No. 8 eases its way across the 517-foot timber span that gave Bear Creek the claim of being one of the largest wooden bridges in the world.—CAM'S PHOTO SERVICE

BRITISH COLUMBIA FOREST PRODUCTS

The railroad operations of British Columbia Forest Products were concentrated in the Cowichan and Renfrew districts of southern Vancouver Island and were formed from the holdings of Industrial Timber Mills Limited, Malahat Logging Company, and the Hemmingsen-Cameron Company.

Industrial Timber Mills' lines fed into a large mill at Youbou, the terminus of Canadian National Railways' Cowichan subdivision. Using the old CNR line from Youbou to the outlet of Cowichan Lake where Nitinat Camp was established, the company was able to exploit some highly productive timber stands to the west and north of the lake. Another separate rail line was operated on the south side of Cowichan Lake at the isolated settlement of Caycuse. Both of these rail lines were ultimately integrated with trucking operations before their final abandonment.

The Malahat Logging Company's line possessed the most spectacular railroad bridge ever constructed on Vancouver Island. It was 254 feet high

This large Lidgerwood loader was operated on BCFP's Nitinat railroad line into the 1950's.—CAM'S PHOTO SERVICE (BELOW) Industrial Timber Mills Limited's 75-ton Climax No. 2 eases past a 120-ton steam skidder near Camp 6 at Cowichan Lake during July 1937. The locomotive was originally built for the Capilano Timber Company in 1918 and ultimately became British Columbia Forest Products No. 3. — BRITISH COLUMBIA FOREST SERVICE

Malahat Logging's big Heisler West Coast Special was an impressive locomotive. Shown here in 1953 as British Columbia Forest Products Ltd.'s No. 8, the machine was nearing the end of its career. — CAM'S PHOTO SERVICE

and spanned some 900 feet across Bear Creek. The loggers claimed that it was the highest wooden trestle in the west. Malahat Logging Company (and later its successor British Columbia Forest Products Limited) also had the distinction of operating the only three-truck Heisler locomotive on Vancouver Island. This machine was a "West Coast Special," the most advanced version of the Heisler produced by the Erie, Pennsylvania, builder and was designed to compete with Lima's Pacific Coast Shay type locomotive.

The other major predecessor of British Columbia Forest Products Limited, the Hemmingsen-Cameron Company, had less call to fame for spectacular structures or unusual locomotives, but did possess a large railroad line running east from Port Renfrew on the north side of the San Juan River

Heading down to Caycuse Camp from South Fork with 20 log cars in tow is a British Columbia Forest Products three-truck Climax. The effects of logging and fires on the landscape are clearly evident in this 1950 photo. — CAM'S PHOTO SERVICE (BELOW) Cowichan Lake was the booming grounds for most of the logging railroads in the Cowichan region. Here Industrial Timber Mills No. 1 pulls past the unloader on the north shore of the lake in 1938. — BRITISH COLUMBIA FOREST SERVICE

Valley. Hemmingsen-Cameron Company succeeded the firm of Cathels and Sorenson in logging this part of the west coast of Vancouver Island.

In all, British Columbia Forest Products Limited had 13 steam locomotives on its roster, including six Shays, the Heisler, and six Climaxes. It was the only company on Vancouver Island that operated all three of the main types of geared locomotives. Interestingly, the company owned no rod locomotives for use on its long main lines. The last steam locomotive owned by the company was Pacific Coast Shay No. 19, scrapped at Youbou in January 1960. Today, one diesel is retained on the roster for switching at the company's large Crofton pulp mill complex.

COMOX LOGGING & RY. CO.

The Comox Logging and Railway Company operates what is probably the most famous of all the logging railroads on Vancouver Island. In 1909, its predecessor, the Comox and Campbell Lake Tramway Company Limited, constructed a logging railroad in the Courtenay area. This firm was a subsidiary of the Fraser River Lumber Company, which operated a large sawmill complex at Fraser Mills on the lower mainland of British Columbia. In 1910, the Fraser River Lumber Company was reincorporated as the Canadian Western Lumber Company, and the railway subsidiary was renamed the Comox Logging and Railway Company. The firm of Foley, Welch and Stewart was contracted to extend the railroad line north from Royston through Courtenay to a camp known as Headquarters. By March 1911, the southerly portion of the line was in operation and the railway was officially opened.

In order to claim the timber in the area, the company was required to build a mill, although the frequency of operation was not stipulated. A large mill was erected at Headquarters near the proposed Campbell River extension of the Esquimalt and Nanaimo Railway. The boilers of the mill were fired up on the day the timber sale was finalized, but it was used only for a short time. In later years, equipment from the mill was salvaged for the Canadian Western Lumber Company's plant at Fraser Mills. The concrete power house at the mill was used to store logging cables and other supplies, and the circular saws were painted and used for novel railway crossing signs. Over the next four decades, Headquarters was the center of

Heading back to the Nanaimo Lakes to pick up another trainload of logs, Comox Logging & Railway's 2-8-2 No. 16, on the opposite page, wheels across Boulder Creek trestle in April 1959. In 1972 and 1973 this locomotive operated on the Victoria Pacific Railway, a tourist service near Victoria, and was eventually moved to Squamish for display.—DAVE WILKIE. (RIGHT) Comox Logging's 2-6-2 No. 1 is dwarfed by the timber it is about to haul. Beginning with the operations of No. 1 in 1909, CL&R trains worked in the woods of the Comox area for over 40 years. (BELOW) Near Comox Lake CL&R's No. 2, a 2-6-2 tank locomotive, works a train of log cars past the Lidgerwood skidder or "flying machine." Comox Logging pioneered the use of high-lead logging techniques on Vancouver Island.—BOTH LEONARD FRANK —PROVINCIAL ARCHIVES

No. 1 was built by the Baldwin Locomotive Works for Comox Logging in 1909, and carried construction number 33561. This little Prairie-type locomotive operated for 34 years before being scrapped in 1943. — LEONARD FRANK — PROVINCIAL ARCHIVES

a vast complex of logging railroads that criss-crossed the hills and coastal plains of the Comox district.

Comox Logging and Railway Company was one of the few operations on Vancouver Island to make extensive use of the Heisler geared locomotive. By 1930, the company had acquired five of these machines to operate on the steeper grades and switchbacks of its lines. The first two, Nos. 4 and 5, were bought new from the Heisler works in 1911 and 1912 respectively. The last three were acquired from the Columbia River Lumber Company at Golden, B. C., and became Comox Logging's Nos. 8, 9, and 10 on their arrival in 1929.

One of these Heislers, the No. 4, had a rather chequered career. On August 18, 1920, it blew up while pushing a train of loaded cars pulled by 2-6-2 No. 3 near the company's Camp 3. Both the engineer and fireman were killed. The boiler reportedly flipped end over end nearly six car lengths down the track before coming to rest. The brakeman was blown free, escaping the wreck. However, he paid a price for his good fortune. At the time of the explosion he was counting a roll of $5 bills in the locomotive cab and the money came raining down all around the wreck. The battered 4 Spot was salvaged and towed away for rebuilding. Placed back in service after repairs were completed, it remained on the Comox Logging roster until 1936, when it was traded to the Alberni Pacific Lumber Company for a small gas locomotive. After being overhauled, the unlucky No. 4 was put to work on the company's China Creek operation. There, on one of its first runs, it ran away on a steep switchback and plunged into a ravine. This time, the engine was a total wreck, and it was never rebuilt.

In the early days, all of the Comox Logging and Railway Company's locomotives burned scrap wood, but after a connection was made with the Wellington Colliery Railway at Royston, a change over to coal was made. In later years, to reduce fire hazard, a final conversion was made and the locomotives burned fuel oil. Needless to say, this last change pleased the firemen.

Comox Logging acquired a varied roster of locomotives during its operations in steam. In addition to the Heislers, four Shays and seven rod engines were employed out of Headquarters Camp and in later years on the company's Nanaimo Lakes line. Three of the Shays were purchased from Merrill Ring Wilson Ltd., which formerly operated logging railroads on both Vancouver Island and the mainland of British Columbia. One of these Shays, the former Comox Logging No. 15, is still in operation as Elk Falls Company No. 1, the last Shay at work for the logging industry.

The company usually maintained between 50 and 75 miles of track in operation at any one time, relaying the spurs as the timber was cut back into the mountains. By the time the railroad operation came to an end in the Comox area, approximately 1,000 miles of twisting, climbing track had been laid. Rail weights varied from 40 pounds on the spurs to 60 pounds on the main line. Grades often reached eight percent, and switchbacks were common.

Heisler No. 10 is shown here crossing the Nanaimo River as work began in the early 1940's to open up the Comox Logging operation in the Ladysmith area. — R. J. KNIGHT COLLECTION

Comox Logging's third locomotive was a husky big-boilered 2-6-2. With a seemingly endless train of loaded flats, No. 3 shoves her load onto the dock at the Royston booming grounds. — LEONARD FRANK PHOTOS (RIGHT) No. 3 steams quietly at Headquarters Camp where it worked from 1911 until it was scrapped in 1944. — LEONARD FRANK — PROVINCIAL ARCHIVES

A water stop for Shay No. 12 gives the engineer an opportunity to apply a little oil to the valve gear. No. 12 was operating on the Nanaimo Lakes line when this 1953 photograph was taken. This locomotive was withdrawn from service in the 1950s when its crankshaft broke. Subsequently it was placed on display at Ladysmith and later moved to Lake Cowichan. —ALBERT FARROW

The steel and timber bridge over the Nanaimo River is the largest on the logging railroad. In this scene, MacMillan Bloedel's No. 1055, which was leased to Comox Logging in 1959 and operated as CL&R No. 19, backs downgrade towards Ladysmith. Both companies operated log trains over this scenic stretch of railroad. — ROBERT D. TURNER

Dieselization of the Comox Logging line to Ladysmith from the Nanaimo Lakes came when Baldwin switcher No. 7128 was acquired in 1960. The 1,000 h.p. diesel was built in 1943 for the United States Army. It is shown here crossing Boulder Creek in August 1969. — Robert D. Turner

After over 40 years of railroading, Comox Logging and Railway Company shut down its Headquarters railroad operation in December 1953 and moved much of its equipment to the newer Nanaimo Lakes line established in 1943. Headquarters passed into history, but the stories of the operations still circulate. The following is an example. The No. 11 had just arrived from Vancouver where it was re-boilered following its purchase from the Donovan Corkery Logging Company. As the story goes, it was a cold November night and the crew had gathered in the cab of the locomotive for the run back to Headquarters from the Royston booming grounds. The big 2-8-2 pulled out of Royston, but as the last two cars were clearing the dump, they derailed. No one in the cab noticed a thing except that the No. 11 seemed a bit sluggish that night. The derailed cars were dragged for miles up the main line, ripping out switches and crossings and anything else in the way. Needless to say, the next day the repair crews were out in force!

Steam railroading continued out of the Nanaimo Lakes Camp throughout the 1950's, until December 1960. At this time, a former United States Army Baldwin 1,000 h.p. diesel switcher replaced Comox Logging's venerable Nos. 11 and 16 on the main line, and they were relegated to standby service. A brief reprieve came for the No. 11 in the winter of 1962 when the diesel required major servicing. Soon after this service, the No. 11 and No. 12, a Shay, were placed on display outside the company's offices at Ladysmith. The old No. 2 had already gone to Courtney for preservation two years before. The No. 16 was sold to the West Coast Rail Fan Association which later leased her to Pacific Tours Limited for operation in excursion service on the Island. The one other surviving Comox Logging steam locomotive is the No. 7, now on display at Squamish, B. C., where it had worked previously for the Howe Sound, Pemberton Valley and Northern Railway, a predecessor to the Pacific Great Eastern Railway.

Shay No. 5 of Canadian Forest Products Ltd. leads a long train of log cars into Englewood on a sunny morning in 1947. The big three-truck Shay locomotive was built in 1925 for the Wood and English Logging Company, one of the pioneer operators on northern Vancouver Island. —Leonard Frank Photos

CANADIAN FOREST PRODUCTS, LTD.

The history of Canadian Forest Products, Ltd., which operates the largest logging railroad in Canada, can be traced back to the days of World War I, when two companies started logging operations in the Nimpkish Valley on northern Vancouver Island. In 1917, the Nimpkish Timber Company built its first railroad lines and began hauling timber from the woods to the coast with two geared engines. Seven years later, the company was renamed Wood and English Logging Company, from which the settlement of Englewood derived its name. In 1918, the Beaver Cove Lumber and Pulp Company constructed a railroad to supply its small sulfite pulp plant and sawmill at Beaver Cove. Because of its remoteness from markets, the operations closed the following year.

In 1926 a new company was formed, based on the purchase of the Beaver Cove Lumber and Pulp Company Limited. The new company was named Canadian Forest Products Limited, whose principal shareholder was the International Harvester Company. Logging and sawmilling operations of the two companies continued sporadically through the depression years. In 1944, the interests of Wood and English Logging Company and Canadian Forest Products Limited were purchased by the present owners of the Canfor Group of Companies and renamed the Englewood Logging Division of Canadian Forest Products, Ltd.

Until 1957, logs were railroaded from backwoods camps in the Nimpkish Valley to the head of Nimpkish Lake, then barged 14 miles down the lake to the reload point of another railroad which continued another twelve miles to tidewater. This operation was costly and inconvenient, but eco-

A Wood and English Logging Company Climax steams past the log dump on May 3, 1926 as the first loads tumble down the log skids into the ocean.—A. A. Paull—Vancouver Public Library

Two of the smaller geared locomotives operating in the Englewood area were Nimpkish Timber Company's Shay No. 1 and 45-ton Climax No. 4 of the Beaver Cover Lumber and Pulp Company shown on the left. Both were photographed in 1928 after their acquisition by Wood and English Logging Company. — Both British Columbia Forest Service

The Wood and English Logging Company, at Englewood on northern Vancouver Island, had an efficient system for unloading logs. In the above view, three carloads hit the water at the same time. Note that the extra long logs are spanned between the end bunks of two empty skeleton cars. (LEFT) The Wood and English mill at Englewood was one of the largest on the northern end of Vancouver Island. These scenes were photographed in June 1926. (OPPOSITE PAGE) Summertime called for spark arresters even on the rainy west coast of British Columbia. Here the shop crew of Wood and English Logging fits Shay No. 5 with a big stack. The 110-ton Shay was one of the largest on Vancouver Island.—ALL A. A. PAULL—VANCOUVER PUBLIC LIBRARY

Canadian Forest Products Limited's 2-6-6-2 No. 111 was the only simple articulated locomotive of this type ever to operate in Canada. No. 111 was originally built for the Weyerhaeuser Timber Company of Longview, Washington. The spotless locomotive is pictured at Woss Camp in 1947. — LEONARD FRANK PHOTOS

The articulation of a large 2-6-6-2 logging locomotive is apparent in this view of No. 111 rounding a tight curve at Woss Camp. — LEONARD FRANK PHOTOS

nomic conditions prevented the long-desired rail link from being started until October 1954. In a little over three years, the 23 mile extension was completed. The total cost was in excess of $2,500,-000.

Over the years, Canadian Forest Products, Ltd. accumulated quite a variety of motive power with ancestry as varied as the engines themselves. The largest engine, the No. 111, a 145-ton 2-6-6-2 Baldwin, came from the Weyerhaeuser Timber Company in Washington. Others came from Merrill Ring Wilson Limited, MacMillan Bloedel Limited, and of course, the earlier companies of Wood and English and Beaver Cove Lumber and Pulp.

Canadian Forest Products No. 113 worked for many years at Port Alberni as Alberni Pacific Lumber Company's No. 6. Later it went to Chemainus and the Copper Canyon line of MacMillan & Bloedel as their first No. 1055. This 135-ton Alco-built 2-8-2 was the last serviceable Canfor steam locomotive. It was used for standby service and company picnics long after log hauling was performed by the company's diesels. After a number of years on display at Woss, it was returned to service between 1988 and 1995 for tours and special runs. Occasional use on log trains gave the 113 the distinction of being the last steam locomotive used in log hauling on Vancouver Island.—BRITISH COLUMBIA FOREST SERVICE

The left side of a Shay is starkly simple compared to the complex drive mechanism on the right side of the boiler. The engineer of No. 5 opens the water valve as the Shay waits for trackage rights at Englewood in 1947. — LEONARD FRANK PHOTOS

Canadian Forest Products No. 117 was fully 40 tons lighter than Shay No. 5 shown above. This three-truck machine was erected by the Lima Locomotive Works in 1913. It was scrapped in Vancouver during March of 1961. — BRITISH COLUMBIA FOREST SERVICE

Pacific Coast Shay No. 115 survived dieselization to operate at North Vancouver before finally being donated to Fort Steele near Cranbrook for preservation. — BRITISH COLUMBIA FOREST SERVICE

Four General Motors 1,200 h.p. diesels, like No. 301 shown above dumping logs, handle nearly all traffic on Canadian Forest Products Ltd.'s modern railroad operation. This rail line, which extends from Englewood one hundred miles back into the Nimpkish Valley, is one of the largest logging railroads in North America. — CANFOR

Diesels gradually took over Canadian Forest Products, Ltd. operations during the late 1950's and early 1960's as the remaining steam locomotives were phased out. Today, only one steam engine, a big Alco 2-8-2, remains serviceable on the company property. This locomotive, the No. 113, is still used on occasional work trains and for company picnics. In October and November, 1971, it made a rare appearance under steam to haul logs between Woss Lake and Nimpkish Camp. This gave the veteran engine the distinction of being the last steam locomotive on Vancouver Island to haul timber over a main line logging railroad.

The diesels on Canadian Forest Products, Ltd.'s line, while not as colorful as the steam locomotives, are some of the most unusual in service anywhere in North America. The Canfor roster included such machines as a 400 h.p. diesel powered Shay and a homemade diesel Climax. At present, the bulk of main line power is provided by four 1,200 h.p. General Motors diesel units.

Framed by the rugged beauty of the mountains of northern Vancouver Island, a Canadian Forest Products Ltd. diesel rumbles over Noomas Creek in the remote Nimpkish Valley.—CANFOR

No. 301 eases a train load of long logs past the loader in a scene framed by a beautiful stand of Douglas fir. Note the tank cars equipped with fire-fighting gear. These cars are included in all trains during the dry summer months. — CANFOR

Locomotive No. 252 is a unique product of the loggers' ingenuity. It is a diesel-powered Climax rebuilt from Beaver Cover Lumber and Pulp Company's 45-ton No. 7. Notice the speeders and the large logs loaded on the cars in the background of this 1963 scene. — BRITISH COLUMBIA FOREST SERVICE

Canadian Forest Products Limited's other unique diesel is No. 98 (subsequently renumbered 251). This machine was built as a standard two-truck Shay in 1921 for Pacific Mills Limited and saw service on a number of logging railroads on the coast before being rebuilt as a diesel by the Tyee Machinery Company in 1951. — CANFOR

37.8

6

A QUARTER CENTURY OF CHANGE

THE LAST QUARTER century has seen many changes to the Island's railways. It has been a time of disappearance and retrenchment in the face of changing technologies, distribution systems and travel needs. In the early 1970s, the overall network of trackage was still largely in place on the major systems and several industrial operations remained active. Since then, a steady erosion of the rail network and the traffic supporting it has occurred. Freight traffic to and from Victoria, for example, has dwindled to just a few cars of propane a week. Between 1980 and the early 1990s, carloads shipped to the Island on the E&N dropped by nearly half. Most remaining traffic is to and from Port Alberni with trains usually running several times a week.

Product distribution has changed greatly in the last 25 years. In the early 1970s, many commodities were shipped directly to wholesalers and larger businesses on the Island by rail in boxcars or refrigerator cars. Subsequently, many industries and larger warehousing operations have closed or moved from the Island. The mainland railways have switched much of their business to intermodal services carrying containers and truck trailers to new facilities in the Vancouver area. From there trucks make deliveries to customers on Vancouver Island.

Aside from terminal operations at pulp and paper mills, industrial railways have all but disappeared. Only one, operated by Canfor on northern Vancouver Island, remains. This is due in part to improvements in trucking technology but it is also a reflection of changing land use on eastern Vancouver Island and the accelerated pace of logging and with it the disappearance of old growth timber. Rail logging was only competitive with trucking in valley lands and these areas have all been extensively logged and in many cases have been fragmented by subdivision and urbanization. Moreover, unsustainable forestry practices in other areas and increased mechanization have meant that many mills have closed and that timber cutting is on a much smaller scale.

Some notable achievements have been made in railway preservation on the Island with laudable projects completed or underway. These include the work of the Western Vancouver Island Industrial Heritage Society at Port Alberni, the restoration of CNR 2-8-0 2141 in Kamloops and the restoration programs of the B.C. Forest Museum at Duncan.

The following sections bring the story of change on Vancouver Island's railways from the early 1970's through to the late 1990's.

As if symbolizing the decline of rail traffic on Vancouver Island, rain glistens off the E&N's empty tracks and truss bridge over the Koksilah River south of Duncan.—ROBERT D. TURNER

CANADIAN PACIFIC'S ESQUIMALT & NANAIMO AND VIA RAIL

The Canadian Pacific's Esquimalt and Nanaimo has changed dramatically in its operations and importance to the Island. Operationally, new locomotives replaced the CPR's pioneer Baldwin roadswitchers in the 1970s. In 1973, the 8012 had an electrical fire, 8005 was damaged in a derailment and later four units were destroyed in a wreck south of Nanaimo. The others were retired by the end of 1975 and were scrapped, except No. 8000 which was preserved by the CPR. The Baldwin yard diesels lasted longer, being retired or sold between 1975 and 1982. A variety of diesels have appeared on the Island including CP Rail's two GP30s but by the mid-1990s GP38ACs and GP38-2s were the mainstays of the service. In 1997, reflecting the decreased levels of traffic, only five of these were assigned to the Island, all operating from Nanaimo.

Although on some parts of the E&N there is little traffic, abandonments have been limited. In November 1984, 18.3 miles of track between Hayward Junction north of Duncan and Lake Cowichan was abandoned and soon scrapped. The log trains that operated to Ladysmith for Crown Zellerbach and later Fletcher Challenge were the major source of traffic in the last years. The Crofton Spur, 2.1 miles, was next to be abandoned in April, 1987. In Victoria, street trackage beyond the passenger station was removed in April 1993 and the diesel switcher moved to the mainland. By 1997, freight traffic south of Duncan was down to a few propane cars each week and only one freight train a week served Courtenay.

As traffic declined, the Victoria terminals were phased out. The roundhouse, one of the few surviving in Canada, is used only by VIA. Although designated a heritage building, the roundhouse is slowly deteriorating and its long term survival is in question. All CPR auxiliary equipment was removed; the steam crane was retired and sold for scrap. However, it was purchased by the Prince George Railway and Forestry Museum and is operated on special occasions. The bunkcar, one of the few surviving Canadian Pacific colonist sleeping cars, was acquired by the West Coast Railway Association at Squamish.

Connections for the E&N at Nanaimo with the mainland are provided by the Canadian Pacific ferries *Carrier Princess* and *Princess Superior* and the charter vessel *Seaspan Doris*. These vessels carry trucks as well as railcars and a service is also run to a truck terminal at Swartz Bay north of Victoria. For many years, service originated at CP Rail's ferry terminal on Burrard Inlet but on October 29, 1995, operations were shifted to a dock on the Fraser River at Tilbury Island and the Coal Harbour facility was dismantled. Rail ferries, including the *Seaspan Greg*, also serve coastal mills on Vancouver Island. In 1996, Seaspan was purchased by Denis Washington, owner of Montana Rail Link and the B.C. Southern Railway.

In 1996, CP Rail Systems reorganized its freight operations on the Island as E&N Railfreight, a separate operating unit, managed by Marty Cove, within the parent company. On March 11, a GP38AC locomotive, No. 3005, repainted in Calgary in an attractive green and yellow scheme, was unveiled at a ceremony in Nanaimo by Edward V. Dodge, executive vice-president of CP Rail Systems and Premier Glen Clark. Later that year, CP Rail Systems was reorganized and renamed the Canadian Pacific Railway, a return to the name so long associated with the company.

The political and legal battles over the fate of the E&N passenger service have continued. The Dayliner has been a perennial political issue and most provincial leaders, regardless of party, have supported it. British Columbia Premiers Van der Zalm and

A new station opened in Victoria for the VIA Dayliners in November 1985. This photo was taken on August 1986 when a celebration marked the centennial of the driving of the last spike for the E&N.—Robert D. Turner

Baldwin diesels dominated the E&N until the early 1970s when they were retired and replaced by General Motors GP9R roadswitchers. One of the last assignments for the Baldwins was log-hauling from Lake Cowichan to Ladysmith. Painted in CP Rail's bright red-orange colors, 8003 leads the 8000 and a long train of empty log flats southbound near Mount Sicker on the way to Lake Cowichan in June 1973. (RIGHT) Baldwin replacement GP9Rs 8692 and 8531 roll a loaded log train northbound near Westholme several years later, just before the Lake Cowichan subdivision was abandoned in 1984.—BOTH ROBERT D. TURNER

Harcourt, as philosophically opposed as two politicians could be, made special trips over the line. However, substantial provincial funding to modernize the service has never been forthcoming.

The story of the Dayliner's survival is a tangled web of local initiatives and court cases. These are a few highlights. After several unsuccessful applications to abandon the service, the railway received permission from the Canadian Transport Commission to stop the trains in 1978. However, on review the decision was reversed. In the meantime, VIA Rail Canada was formed in 1977 to take over nearly all passenger services in Canada and in 1979 VIA assumed responsibility for the Dayliner.

Prompted in no small measure by local supporters and community groups, subsequent improvements to the service included a new station in downtown Victoria and new shelters at several communities. During the summer as many as three RDCs have been used on the daily trains. There have been variations in the schedules to encourage weekend travel and special ski trains have been run to Courtenay. In winter, one RDC is used on the trains.

However, in 1989 the Federal Government moved to shut down the service prompting a suit by the province. In 1991 the B.C. Supreme Court ruled in favour of the province but on appeal to the Supreme Court of Canada, the federal government's position was upheld. The court ruled on May 5, 1994 that the service did not need to be maintained, based on the

Southbound E&N Dayliners clear Hayward Junction as the crew of a Lake Cowichan subdivision way-freight waits to take the mainline north to Nanaimo in 1978.—Robert D. Turner

The *Seaspan Doris*, formally the *Doris Yorke*, is one of the railcar ferries connecting the E&N with CPR mainland operations.—Robert D. Turner

original agreements by the governments and the Esquimalt and Nanaimo Railway.

Nonetheless, VIA continued to operate the Dayliners, or the *Railiners* as VIA calls the RDCs, through the summer of 1997. However, early in 1997, David Anderson, then the Minister of Transport, made it clear that the present level of subsidy was unsustainable. At the same time, multi-billion dollar reconstruction of the Island Highway was underway making the railway, with its 19th and early 20th-century engineering, even less competitive.

The E&N's huge land grants, which came under CPR control, remain a contentious point in public discussions over the fate of the railway and the passenger service. The land grants, it is often argued, despite the court decisions, were provided to fund the operation of the railway. To many people, the Dayliner is the railway and the moves to discontinue the passenger operations are perceived as being the same as a move to abandon the entire railway. With the continuing decline in freight traffic, the loss of the Dayliner could well lead to the abandonment of remaining freight services except probably those between Nanaimo and Port Alberni.

Dayliner service was expanded in June 1980 when VIA assigned three RDC's to the Island. On June 3, the first day of three-car operation, a well patronized train crossed Arbutus Canyon.—DAVE WILKIE

3005 3005
E&N

CANADIAN NATIONAL RAILWAYS

Canadian National's services on Vancouver Island dwindled and then disappeared in the 1970s and 1980s. A tourist railway, using former Comox Logging 2-8-2 No. 16 and two coaches, operated in the summers of 1972 and 1973 on the CNR near Colwood, but the lease was terminated and the operation ceased. At Ogden Point, the grain elevator, which received large numbers of grain cars by rail barge, was closed in 1976 but the rail yard continued to serve as a reload point for lumber exports. For a short time, switching services at Ogden Point were taken over by Westcan Terminals using a Plymouth diesel from Western Forest Industries. However, rail service ended in 1987.

CNR abandoned service south of Deerholme to Rocky Point in 1979, the only traffic remaining being some poles and occasional shipments to the Canadian Forces. The line between Deerholme, Youbou and Cowichan Bay continued to serve the mill at Youbou for another decade until permission was granted for abandonment effective April 1, 1988. Traffic had fallen from about 300 carloads a year in the early 1980s to just 70 cars in 1986. Lumber shipments from Doman Industries at Cowichan Bay also fell to very low levels with most traffic moving by truck and ferry to the Burlington Northern in New Westminster. Losses for 1986 were estimated at $885,000.

At left, showing off its E&N Railfreight colors, GP38AC 3005 leads 3007, painted for CP Rail Systems, and 3006 in CP Rail's older colors over the summit of the Port Alberni subdivision westbound in June 1996. (ABOVE) The crew of CNR veteran roadswitcher 1003 switches just two boxcars on the *Seaspan Greg* in Victoria on June 29, 1987. The once busy harbour, which was surrounded by mills and shipyards, evolved into an area dominated by condominiums and hotels.—BOTH ROBERT D. TURNER

Canadian National's traffic all but disappeared by the 1980s. On March 27, 1988, with the last train from Youbou, the 1000 is ready to leave with six bulkhead flats, only partly loaded because of the deteriorated tracks, and a caboose. The caboose was dropped off at Lake Cowichan for preservation. (BELOW) CN's 1003 slowly crosses the Selkirk trestle with two cars for Johnston Terminals on April 15, 1985. The 1,966-foot trestle has been rebuilt as part of a pedestrian and bicycle trail to Victoria.—Both Dave Wilkie

The isolated trackage in Victoria also saw a steady erosion of traffic. The BC Forest Products mill, which in the late 1980s shipped between 60 and 100 carloads of large timbers, plywood and lumber a year, closed and Johnston Terminals, once an important shipper, converted its operations to trucking as did other businesses. CN ended its chartered ferry service to Victoria and Cowichan Bay when its contract with Seaspan, using the *Seaspan Greg*, expired in 1988. Traffic to Victoria was handled over the E&N and interchanged with CN until finally, on January 5, 1990, the last grain car was switched from Borden Mercantile, the last customer, and the line was abandoned.

The CNR's right-of-way was acquired by the BC government and several sections have been developed as an outstanding system of walking and cycling trails. In 1996, the lift span over the Gorge waterway was reconstructed as part of this system providing a key link between the city and suburban areas. At the same time, CNR No. 2141, which had been one of the last CN steam locomotives on Vancouver Island, is being restored by the 2141 Steam Locomotive Restoration Society in Kamloops.

LOGGING AND INDUSTRIAL RAILWAYS

By the late 1990s, only one logging railway survived on Vancouver Island and it is also one of the last in North America. Canadian Forest Products continues to haul logs by rail through the Nimpkish Valley to Beaver Cove using four diesels in an efficient system. Canfor's last operational steam locomotive, 2-8-2 No. 113, used occasionally in the 1970s and then placed on display, was returned to service in 1988 and used for tours of the company's operations through the summer of 1995 after which it was again displayed.

MacMillan Bloedel retired its last steam locomotive, No. 1055, at Chemainus in 1973 and the large mill, built to handle old-growth logs, was dismantled. A smaller mill was built near the site. All four surviving steam locomotives were preserved. No. 1077, restored for use on the Provincial Museum Train between 1975 and 1979 and featured in several movies, was eventually moved to Fort Steele Heritage Park near Cranbrook for continued use. Locomotives 1044 and 1066 were placed on display and 1055 finally went to Port Alberni for restoration as Alberni Pacific No. 7.

With the aid of two secondhand diesels, Crown Zellerbach's logging railway at Ladysmith survived until 1984. By that time, Crown Zellerbach Canada had been purchased by New Zealand-owned Fletcher Challenge and the operations renamed Crown Forest Products. In 1984 a fire damaged the Nanaimo River bridge and closed the railroad. The fire only hastened the end because the timber supply was all but gone in the area and even truck logging ceased soon after. Following the closure, much equipment, including the home-built log unloader, was donated to preservation societies. Subsequently, a railroad museum operated at Ladysmith in the shop buildings for several years before closing.

Forest industry companies still operate four terminal railways on Vancouver Island. The pulp and paper mills at Crofton and Duncan Bay have railways that are served by rail barges from the mainland. These mills, once owned by B.C. Forest Products and Crown Zellerbach respectively, were acquired by Fletcher Challenge Canada Ltd. MacMillan Bloedel's Harmac Pacific pulp and paper mill near Nanaimo has a barge slip and terminal railway and at the company's Port Alberni pulp and paper mill a switcher is used to interchange cars with the Esquimalt and Nanaimo Railway.

Recent preservation efforts have seen three Vancouver Island steam locomotives returned to operation. In 1995, former Mayo Lumber Company No. 3, which had been preserved at the BC Forest Museum, was fully restored for the Kettle Valley Steam Railway at West Summerland in the Okanagan. In Ottawa, the National Museum of Science and Technology, through the efforts of many volunteers, completed restoration of Shay No. 1, acquired from Crown Zellerbach's Elk Falls Company mill at Duncan Bay north of Campbell River. At Port Alberni, the Western Vancouver Island Industrial Heritage Society has restored Alberni Pacific Lumber No. 7, last operated in the early 1970s as MacMillan Bloedel No. 1055 at Chemainus. It was returned to weekend excursion service in the summer of 1996. The society also carried out a beautiful restoration of the Port Alberni E&N station and is working on several other major projects.

Two Canadian Forest Products diesels are ready to leave the Camp A reload in August 1988.—Robert D. Turner (BELOW) MacMillan Bloedel's SW900 No. 16 is typical of locomotives used in several major mills. This diesel came from the Southern Pacific as No. 1197 in 1987. It was photographed at Port Alberni on February 19, 1994.—Dave Wilkie

Crown Zellerbach's 4097, an Alco RS-3 from the Delaware & Hudson acquired in 1973, rumbles past the interlocking tower just north of Ladysmith in the summer of 1977 with logs from the Nanaimo Lakes. The water car sprinkled the right-of-way during the forest fire season. This locomotive and No. 8427, a similar CPR Montreal Locomotive Works unit with a modified short hood, purchased in 1980, handled traffic on the railway until its closure in 1984. The old Baldwin diesel, No. 7128, was transferred to the Elk Falls pulp mill replacing Shay No. 1, which was donated to the National Museum of Science and Technology in Ottawa. In 1986, No. 4097 also was moved to Elk Falls and was eventually preserved at Squamish. The 7128, after a brief respite at Ladysmith, was scrapped and the 8427 is preserved at Port Alberni. (ABOVE RIGHT) Two of Canfor's General Motors' diesels ease across the Noomas River bridge on August 26, 1988. Two SW1200RS locomotives acquired in 1956, a third unit bought in 1959 and a forth purchased second-hand from Georgia Pacific, work on the last logging railway on Vancouver Island. Even after four decades of hard service they are well maintained and productive.—ROBERT D. TURNER

THE YEARS AHEAD

The outlook for the surviving rail operations on Vancouver Island is tenuous. In its present form, the VIA Dayliner service, with aging equipment and little promotion, is certainly operating on borrowed time. Suburban service or commuter trains may be part of the future but funding remains an obstacle that will be hard to overcome. For the E&N between Nanaimo and Port Alberni, there will be a future as long as paper shipments continue and for the present at least, the logging railway of Canadian Forest Products provides a key link in the company's log hauling operations. Otherwise, a few industrial switchers will continue to service large mills but any other development will be in an expansion of preserved railways and tourist operations for which there is great potential, particularly over sections of the E&N. In increasingly congested urban areas, light rail transit systems offer considerable advantages from many perspectives.

In the end, the branch lines and the industrial railways that had been built, often with such difficulty, and opened with such fanfare, disappeared rather quietly. Crucial though they once were to a hundred logging camps, a dozen coal mines and thousands of settlers and travellers, they could not survive or adapt to the accelerating pace of technological and social change that swept by them during the mid-1900s. They were instrumental in their times and often the catalysts for changes that eventually led to their own demise.

BIBLIOGRAPHY

Audain, James. 1964. *Alex Dunsmuir's Dilemma*, Sunnylane Publishing Co., Victoria, B.C.

Barr, Ira E. 1940. "Early Locomotives on Vancouver Island," *British Columbia Historical Quarterly*, April, pp. 134-36.

British Columbia Railway Historical Association. 1960. *Canadian Forest Products*, Bulletin No. 2, British Columbia Railway Historical Association, Victoria, BC.

Clegg, Anthony, and Ray Corley. 1969. *Canadian National Steam Power*, Trains & Trolleys Publishing Co., Montreal, PQ.

Clyne, J. V. 1964. *What's Past is Prologue: The History of MacMillan Bloedel and Powell River Limited*, MacMillan Bloedel Ltd., Vancouver, BC.

DeCosmos, Amor. 1880. *Island Railway Papers*, Queen's Printers, Ottawa, ON.

Flemming, Sanford. 1874. *Canadian Pacific Railway: Report of the Explorations and Surveys up to January 1874*, MacLean, Rogers and Co., Ottawa, ON.

———. 1877. *Report on Surveys and Preliminary Operations on the Canadian Pacific Railway*. MacLean, Rogers and Co., Ottawa, ON.

———. 1878. *Canadian Pacific Railway: Report and Documents in Reference to the Canadian Pacific Railway*. MacLean, Rogers and Co., Ottawa, ON.

Harvey, R. D. 1960. *History of Saanich Peninsula Railways*, Queen's Printer, Victoria, BC.

Hearn, George and David Wilkie. 1966. *The Cordwood Limited*, British Columbia Railway Historical Association, Victoria, BC.

Johnson, Arthur J. 1936. *The Canadian Pacific Railway and British Columbia, 1871-1886*, Unpublished Master of Arts Thesis, University of British Columbia, Vancouver, BC.

Koch, Michael. 1971. *The Shay Locomotive, Titan of the Timber*, World Press, Denver, CO.

Lavallée, Omer, S. A. and Robert R. Brown. 1951. Locomotives of the Canadian Pacific Railway Company, *Bulletin* 83, Railway & Locomotive Historical Society, Boston, MA.

Macfie, Matthew. 1865. *Vancouver Island and British Columbia*, Longman, Green Ltd., London, England.

Maiden, Cecil. 1948. *Lighted Journey*, British Columbia Electric Railway, Vancouver, BC.

Mount Sicker & Brenton Mines, Ltd. 1901. *Prospectus*, Victoria, BC.

Myers, T. R. 1954. *Ninety Years of Public Utility Service*, British Columbia Electric Railway, Vancouver, BC.

Norcross, E. B. and D. F. Tonkin. 1969. *Frontier Days of Vancouver Island*, Island Books, Courtenay, BC.

Poor, Henry V. 1875-1924. *Manual of Railroads*, M. V. Poor Co., New York, NY.

Ranger, Dan, Jr. 1964. *Pacific Coast Shay*, Golden West Books, San Marino, CA.

Roberts, Joseph. 1937. *The Origins of the Esquimalt and Nanaimo Railway: A Problem in British Columbia Politics.* Unpublished Master of Arts Thesis, University of British Columbia, Vancouver, BC.

Solly, L. H. 1914. *The Timber, Agricultural and Industrial Resources of Vancouver Island.* Esquimalt & Nanaimo Railway, Victoria, BC.

Stevens, G. R. 1962. *Canadian National Railways, Vol. 2, Towards the Inevitable*, Clarke, Irwin & Co., Toronto, ON.

Swanson, Robert E. 1960. *A History of Railroad Logging*, Queen's Printer, Victoria, BC.

White, Elwood, 1959. *Roster of Vancouver Island Logging Railways*, British Columbia Railway Historical Association, Victoria, BC.

White, Elwood and David Wilkie. 1964. *Shays on the Switchbacks*, British Columbia Railway Historical Association, Victoria, BC.

In addition, information was drawn from the Annual Reports of the BC Department of Commercial Transport (1960-1970), the BC Department of Mines (1874-1962), and the BC Department of Railways (1911-1924, 1945-1958). Trade journals and magazines consulted included: *The British Columbia Lumberman*, *Pacific News*, *Railroad Magazine*, *The Steam Chest*, *The Timberman*, and *Trains*. BC Newspapers reviewed included: *Comox District Free Press*, Courtenay; the *Cowichan Leader*, Duncan; *Nanaimo Free Press*, Nanaimo; *The Daily Colonist*, Victoria; *The Province*, Vancouver; *The Vancouver Sun*, Vancouver; and *The Victoria Daily Times*, Victoria.

Since *Vancouver Island Railroads* was published in 1973 a number of books have been released that provide further information on the rail operations and related topics. I have expanded on the information in *Vancouver Island Railroads* particularly in *Logging by Rail* and there are several sections on the E&N in *West of the Great Divide*, including an E&N locomotive roster. *The Pacific Princesses* provides a history of the CPR's British Columbia Coast Steamship Service. Additional references are included in all of these books.

Bohi, Charles W. and Leslie S. Kozma. 1993. *Canadian Pacific's Western Depots*, South Platte Press, David City, NE.

Cail, Robert E. 1974. *Land, Man, and the Law, The Disposal of Crown Lands in British Columbia, 1871-1913*, University of British Columbia Press, Vancouver, BC.

Dean, Murray W. and David B. Hana. 1981. *Canadian Pacific Diesel Locomotives*, Railfare /Fitzhenry & Whiteside, Don Mills, ON.

Eagle, John A. 1989. *The Canadian Pacific Railway and the Development of Western Canada*, McGill-Queen's University Press, Kingston, ON.

Ewert, Henry. 1986. *The Story of the B.C. Electric Railway Company*, Whitecap Books, North Vancouver, BC.

———. 1992. *Victoria's Streetcar Era*, Sono Nis Press, Victoria, BC.

Green, Mervyn T. 1987. *British Columbia Industrial Locomotives*, Published by the author, Richmond, BC.

Lamb, W. Kaye. 1977. *A History of the Canadian Pacific Railway*, Collier-Macmillan. New York, NY.

Lavallée, Omer. 1985. *Canadian Pacific Steam Locomotives*, Railfare, Toronto, ON.

MacLachlan, Donald. 1986. *The Esquimalt & Nanaimo Railway. The Dunsmuir Years: 1884-1905*, British Columbia Railway Historical Association, Victoria, BC.

McKnight, George. 1996. *Sawlogs on Steel Rails, 45 Years of Alberni Railway Logging*, Forest Industry Seniors' History Committee, Port Alberni, BC.

Muralt, Darryl. 1992. *V&S, The Victoria & Sidney Railway*, British Columbia Railway Historical Association, Victoria, BC.

Parker, Douglas. 1981. *No Horsecars in Paradise, A History of the Street Railways and Public Utilities in Victoria, B.C. before 1897*, Railfare, Toronto, ON.

Reksten, Terry. 1991. *The Dunsmuir Saga,* Douglas & McIntyre, Vancouver, BC.

Regehr, T. D. 1976. *The Canadian Northern Railway, Pioneer Road of the Northern Prairies,* Macmillan, Toronto, ON.

Roberts, Earl R. and David P. Stremes (editors). 1997. *Canadian Trackside Guide 1997*, Bytown Railway Society, Ottawa, ON.

Turner, Robert D. 1977. *The Pacific Princesses, An Illustrated History of the Canadian Pacific Railway's Princess Fleet on the Northwest Coast,* Sono Nis Press, Victoria, BC.

——. 1981. *Railroaders, Recollections from the Steam Era in British Columbia*, Provincial Archives of British Columbia, Victoria, BC.

——. 1981. "Logging Railroads and Locomotives in British Columbia: A Background Summary and the Preservation Record," *Material History Bulletin,* No. 13, National Museum of Man, Ottawa, ON.

——. 1984. *Pacific Coast Logging* (a series of articles including equipment drawings from Vancouver Island and photos) *Railroad Model Craftsman*, Jan.–Apr. 1984.

——. 1987. *West of the Great Divide, the Canadian Pacific Railway in British Columbia, 1880-1986*, Sono Nis Press, Victoria, BC.

——. 1989. "Three Railways Through Saanich," in Geoffrey Castle (Ed.), *Saanich, An Illustrated History*, The Corporation of the District of Saanich, Victoria, BC.

——. 1990. *Logging by Rail, The B.C. Story*, Sono Nis Press, Victoria, BC.

Young, Cameron. 1986. *The Forests of British Columbia*, Whitecap Books, North Vancouver, BC.

Zuters, Gary, 1994. *CP Rail, 1993 Review*, Hyrail, Ferndale, WA.

Mayo Lumber's wood-burning Shay No. 3, shown at Paldi in 1951, was displayed for many years at Duncan's B.C. Forest Museum. In 1995 it was restored for the Kettle Valley Steam Railway at West Summerland.—AUTHOR'S COLLECTION

Alberni Pacific's *2-Spot* was displayed for three decades in Port Alberni. The Western Vancouver Island Industrial Heritage Society, in co-operation with the Alberni Valley Museum, restored the old Shay to operation in 1984. A deteriorated boiler forced its retirement in 1994. (LEFT) In 1996, after nearly 25 years of inactivity, MacMillan Bloedel's 1055 was returned to operation by the society as Alberni Pacific Lumber No. 7. The big Baldwin 2-8-2T began its career with Campbell River Timber before working for APL and later MacMillan Bloedel. It runs on E&N trackage along the waterfront and posed for this portrait on June 29, 1996.—BOTH DAVE WILKIE

Three units heading for Port Alberni, led by the newly-repainted No. 3005, cross the Englishman River Bridge in June 1996. (RIGHT) Southbound VIA Dayliners roll across Arbutus Canyon on a late afternoon in July 1996.—BOTH ROBERT D. TURNER

INDEX

*This symbol after a page number indicates a photograph of the subject mentioned.

A low winter sun casts long shadows across the yard at Chemainus as MacMillan Bloedel's Porter-built, 2-6-2T No. 1044, eases a long train of empty skeleton cars into a siding above the steep grade leading down to the log dump. A crispness in the air on this beautiful December day in 1968 makes the exhaust steam linger and the whistles echo sharply from the distant hills. In the morning, the cars will be taken by an Esquimalt and Nanaimo crew to Ladysmith. There they will be turned over to MacMillan Bloedel's 1055 and hauled back over the logging railroad running deep into the Nanaimo River valley for more logs. It is the end of a long day and engineer Bob Strang and fireman Onni Parta will soon park their locomotive beside the water tank for the night. Steam railroading will survive for just over a year until this, the last all-steam logging show, will be closed down.—Robert D. Turner